Time's Bounty

Time's Bounty

RETHINKING OLD AGE

TIME'S BOUNTY

PHILIP WEINSTEIN

GODINE • BOSTON

Published in 2025 by
GODINE
Boston, Massachusetts

LIBRARY OF CONGRESS CATALOGING-IN-PUBLICATION DATA
Names: Weinstein, Philip, 1940- author.
Title: Time's bounty / Philip Weinstein.
Description: Boston, Massachusetts : Godine, 2025.
Identifiers: LCCN 2025013466 (print) | LCCN 2025013467 (ebook)
ISBN 9781567928440 (hardcover) | ISBN 9781567928457 (epub)
Subjects: LCSH: Old age—Psychological aspects. | Aging.
Classification: LCC HQ1061 .W385 2025 (print) | LCC HQ1061 (ebook)
DDC 305.26—dc23/eng/20250616
LC record available at https://lccn.loc.gov/2025013466
LC ebook record available at https://lccn.loc.gov/2025013467

Book design by Natalie C. Sousa
Images used under license from Adobe Stock

First Printing, 2025
Printed in the United States of America

For Penny

CONTENTS

PREFACE

Why write a book about old age? My professional training has nothing to do with gerontology. I have had a rewarding career as an English professor for well over forty years, and my publications—eight books and a goodly number of scholarly articles—have all taken the form of literary criticism. Faulkner, Proust, Kafka, Joyce; Dickens and Eliot; Hardy, James, and Conrad: the work of these and other writers has been my abiding subject. Essentially, I have written *as* a scholar and *for* other scholars: a discrete world of experts sharing a cluster of intellectual and linguistic orientations. We collectively labored to produce an intricate scholarly discourse, freed forever from the norms and constraints of ordinary language.

When it was good, it was wonderful indeed: professional recognition is no small thing. But the good of that arrangement began eventually to play out, and as it did so, I took the measure—increasingly, uncomfortably—of the arrangement's cost. I saw that, throughout my academic life—from my thirties into my seventies—I had worked hard to keep my writing clear of my own experience. Although I could not have written a word without tapping into an irrepressible reservoir of personal thoughts and feelings, I had done my best to keep these out of my prose. The writers whose work I loved—and sought to illuminate—were my purpose and my point. Essentially, I was to function as scribe—a sort of "medium" for articulating their beautiful effects onto paper.

As I approached retirement, the omissions troubling these thoughts—that I had devoted my life to a kind of writing that ignored both my own depths and those of my readers—came to a head. I could not help seeing that I would—soon enough—be heading toward my grave, without having tried to explore or set down for others the burden of my thoughts and feelings. Those stances that lived deepest inside me—my "quick" itself, my indwelling take on life—would remain speechless. To keep all this inside and unsaid felt intolerable.

And then everything changed. My fellow travelers, I realized, were no longer other scholars of literature. Nor need the language I could deploy remain the fraught, professional discourse shared by like-minded experts. I saw that I now belonged to a radically different social group: the world of the aged and aging. Your first thought may be: how awful to see yourself in that mirror! In the following pages, I aim to show you otherwise—that this is a world less of depletion than of vital surprises. But to return to my immediate point: I was now grasping my newfound membership in a vast and *democratic* network: all of us in the boat of life itself, as it moves through the turbulent later chapters.

The liberation thus launched would be hard to overstate. In what follows, I make all that I can of the personal (rather than attempting to repress it). I do so because, wherever my narrative goes—into memorial services, nursing homes, doctors' offices, literary narratives of aging and discovery, the morning ritual of coffee in bed—it is never just personal. Other people have had these experiences or will have them; I am always in potential company; the mirror is capacious. Moreover, literature—my lifelong field of professional attention—has hardly been banished from these pages. But it functions differently here. No longer the all-compelling subject of my argument, it is the argument's magnifier, depth-provider, meaning-extender. Its task is to make my book's narratives of old age as resonant as possible. Its aim is to enrich and enlarge the connection between you and me.

To earn and keep your trust, I need to work with language that we all understand.

It was not only I and my calling that changed upon retirement. The reality of time itself changed for me as well. No longer elastic and inexhaustible—a colorless neutral medium within which I would continue my forward-moving career—time began to flaunt its colors and reveal its fickleness. By way of embodied examples increasingly near to me, time was showing me that it could run out altogether. Its passage was becoming a thing of fascination, and I suddenly understood that I had a book on my hands: a book about the passage of time shaping the dramas of the old. In these newfound dramas, what lies behind matters as much as what lies ahead. My task in the following pages is to stage a reckoning with time's passage, and the most resonant term I can find for that reckoning is *bounty*. We now enter the realm of *Time's Bounty*.

Bounty means a number of things—many involving money. But the meanings that course through this book of reckoning center on bounty as *gift* and as *yield*, like the yield (even when unwanted) of a crop we had not known we were sowing or reaping. What unexpected harvest has the passage of time brought forth? At age eighty-four, it is time to take the measure.

I call them "dramas of the old," and I need to say why *drama* is the right term. *Drama* rather than lament or complaint about where we old ones are; *drama* rather than fantasies that pretend we are not where we are. *Drama* functions here as an umbrella-term for the sudden arrival and expression of late-stage thoughts, feelings, and actions—the range of unanticipated life-moves made by the elderly. "Unanticipated" because we never before knew we would make such moves—and this because we never before had to make them. Surprise runs through these pages: do we ever get used to what life puts in our path?

Each of my five chapters narrates one such "drama of winter." Although all five draw on my arrival into a territory that old age seems to mark out as its own, these are not the predictable stories you might anticipate. As mentioned before, no complaints run through my chapters (no "organ recital" is on offer). No sentimental sweetness gets indulged either (the kind of thing that Hallmark cards specialize in). Those seeking to commiserate with a litany of old age's problems—or longing for a Mr.-Chips-like transcendence of them—will need to look elsewhere. Rather, my aim is to press hard on familiar scenarios, hard enough to make them reveal their surprises. I may go to expected places, but I come upon unexpected findings.

"The Mother of Beauty" explores how a number of old-age situations, assumed to announce the end-of-the-road, actually generate fresh life-moves. As we age, we tend to become "lighter" in more senses than one. Yes, we often find ourselves caught up in bodies that have shrunk in weight, height, and appeal. But, once retired, we are also freed of the projects that used to define us—and are strangely permitted (when not required) to change our ways. Indeed, we may find ourselves catapulted into late-stage "adventures" the young never dream of.

"Less" sheds light on the *lessening* of fundamental orientations and resources (previously taken for granted) that comes with age—less work, less sleep, less health. These versions of "less"—this fraying of the fabric of our taken-for-granted selfhood—arrive, moreover, in an American setting awash in the values of the young. An American setting incorrigibly in search of *more*.

"Dormancy" enacts a shift in perspective. Rather than the surprises that old age springs upon us, it focuses on the long-simmering preparations that eventuate into the "bounties" (often unwanted) of life's last chapters. I explore the drama of slumbering conditions (in the body, in the mind) coming awake. Old age appears here as the setting where chickens of every sort—the familiar as well as the strange—come home to roost. From the curse of cancer and Parkinson's to the advent of a new self-reckoning, these proceed by way of dormancy—the unremarkable passage of great chunks of "sleep-time"—as the precondition for dramatic emergence.

A book centered on old age has no choice but to confront "The Thing Itself"—Shakespeare's phrase (from *King Lear*) for the unaccommodated human being at the end of the rope, reduced to "a poor, bare, forked animal." Yet this dire situation—the fate of all bodies—accommodates (in the work of Beckett and Proust) the most provocative seasonings of comedy and pathos. Although all living creatures die, the poet W. B. Yeats noted, only "man has created death." Only human beings foresee, name, and creatively conceptualize what is coming their way: not just dying (an organic event) but the phenomenon of death (a metaphysical mystery).

"Free"—my last chapter—celebrates a ritual of daily release occurring within a familiar domestic setting, one where the realities of a retired elderly couple would seem to impose constraint rather than permit release. After all, two old people drinking coffee together in bed for thirty or forty-five minutes each morning, engaged in desultory conversation before rising to confront the new day: what, you may wonder, is emancipatory about *that*?

In sum, on offer here is a mapping of the unexpected dramas that old age springs upon us, seen without complaint or evasion. Nevertheless, I concede that I embark on this journey with some trepidation. Most of us envisage life's last chapters with anxiety. We do not want to go there in reality and may wonder why we should go there in advance, in our reading. It would be wise to see beyond these hesitations. Current actuarial data stares us in the face. We are living longer lives. Willy-nilly, more and more of us are destined to inhabit this unfamiliar territory for quite a stretch.

That is a cautionary reason for taking the journey with me, but the deeper reason is far from cautionary. There are upsurges of life awaiting us in these later stages—strange discoveries, sudden awakenings, as we come nearer to the ending. And more: these "adventures" may speak compellingly to the younger as well. After all, old age is a realm most of us first encountered when we were still infants. Grandparents, perhaps great-grandparents:

how different from us they were then! No less, though, they speechlessly embodied the human reality that we are, all of us, immersed in the great game of life-in-time.

So I invite you, by way of my five chapters, to take a trip you have likely never read about (even if you are living there), into a terrain whose living topography differs resonantly from preconceptions. "The past is a foreign country," L. P. Hartley wrote in his novel *The Go-Between*. The future (where we are headed) is more foreign yet. I am no expert guide, but I possess the requisite age. Not by choice, I am becoming familiar with nooks and crannies of wintry landscapes. These are vastly more interesting than anything I anticipated. That is why no nostalgic requiem—the gathered pathos of the vanished years—courses through my chapters. They circulate, instead, around drama where least expected. They center not on depletion but on an unpredictable redirecting of life-energies, as these rise to confront the hazards heading toward us.

THE MOTHER OF BEAUTY

Death is the mother of beauty; hence from her,
Alone, shall come fulfilment to our dreams
And our desires.

—WALLACE STEVENS, "SUNDAY MORNING"

These haunting lines by Wallace Stevens promise more than I have ever managed to understand about death: that it shall bring "fulfilment to our dreams / And our desires." By contrast, the beauty I have come to discover in endgame scenarios has nothing to do with dreams and desires. Quite the opposite: it is rather that old age's stark unfoldings—long dreaded as disabling, feared as surcease itself—may nevertheless carry a creative charge that you could not possibly imagine before arriving there. The kind of beauty that emerges is generated not by fulfilment, but rather by an opposing dynamic of change, exposure, the threat of collapse.

Put otherwise, becoming old—approaching death—opens onto unanticipated scenarios that are *interesting*. Not ethically satisfying—nothing enabling or "rewarding" is happening here—yet aesthetically compelling: emergent dramas that strike you with their undeniable cogency, their "rightness." When the philosopher Friedrich Nietzsche claimed (in *The Birth of Tragedy*) that existence can be justified only on aesthetic grounds, he was acknowledging that other criteria for justifying life come up short. Unmastered change is life's keynote; with the final change we cease to exist. Though life may not ultimately come to mean anything, Nietzsche surmised, its passage generates remarkable beauty along the way—and in special ways as the end approaches. In fact, however macabre this sounds, our journey toward extinction throbs with *interest*. Nietzsche imagines the enjoyment the gods might derive from observing the human comedy; life's last chapters exert a bizarre attraction all their own. These are some of the wintry dramas I seek to shed light on.

A distinction associated with another philosopher, Martin Heidegger, may provide further guidance. Though Heidegger can be notoriously difficult, his distinctions sometimes simply hit home. The one I have in mind is the distinction between objects unthinkingly available for use—what he calls the "ready-to-hand"—and objects that have ceased to be useful and have become what he calls the "present-at-hand." Heidegger himself relishes the resourcefulness of our "ready-to-hand" world. His focus is on our ongoing deployment of a furnished and to-be-acted-upon world—on how we go about, moment by moment, making our world *work* for us. Which is great: until it stops. That is the point at which what is "ready-to-hand" becomes—oddly, suddenly—merely "present-at-hand." Just *there*. In so doing, it announces one of old age's compelling dramas: the drama of no longer being able to make things work. Yet this is precisely the moment when the elements that have long made up our ambient world (ultimately: our body itself) may become luminous—as only elements shorn of their previous functionality can become luminous. Old age involves our passage from an unthinking resourcefulness (where we just continue to "get on with it") to a speculative space where nothing can be taken for granted: a space of recurrent radiance.

WINTRY FORMS OF BEAUTY

The role of death as generator of human values is well known. A bedrock reason we care for others is our half-repressed lifelong awareness that neither we nor they will be here forever. Time's passage creates human value in the wake of its positing losses to come. Our creativity is hardwired to our premonition, however muffled, that we will eventually cease to be.

But death's approach generates, as well, a less familiar set of dramas. Involving the beset and failing will, these differ from the projects of our earlier years. Those projects—typically centering on maturation, courtship, family, work, career—focused on *becoming*. As Nietzsche put it in another context, each of them was "pregnant with a future." It would be hard *not* to think of our ongoing life as a narrative composed of challenges encountered and taken on—with rewards (of one form or another) anticipated in the offing. This is a developmental narrative of coming through the storm and finding ourselves renewed. Versions of this story underwrite most of the novels that we read, the movies that we see. However variable the form of this story, its motor is the individual will. Its bedrock premise is a recovered capacity that follows initial setbacks.

But think instead of the dinner party where you hear of the trip gone irreparably wrong because of COVID, the stroke that suddenly occurred, the cancer just diagnosed, the onset of Alzheimer's. These stories center on bodies no longer doing the bidding of the will, on minds going gamey as well. Whatever beauty obtains here has little to do with a pregnant future. We already know what future awaits. To take a lesser example: think of old people walking, trying not to fall even as they know that eventually they will slip up and fall. If you ask, when did *walking* take on the interest of a (modest, daily) drama, the answer is that—as with Heidegger's faulty hammer that compels attention only when it ceases to work—walking compels attention when it ceases to be an unthinking capacity. When it reconfigures as a potentially troublesome activity, requiring care. No longer the automatic moves one makes en route toward somewhere else, walking becomes uncertain as such, an activity newly fraught with risk. Its interest resides not in getting something accomplished, but rather in our newly mandated thinking about ourselves as figures caught out in unmastered motion—and heading toward the fall. What could differ more from the will-directed shaping of a self, the coordination of resources in the pursuit of a goal?

These ominous little dramas generate new forms of thought and feeling all their own. When I spoke to a friend of mine (and close to my age) about the strange thoughts that our bodily infirmities give rise to, he recalled one of John Updike's late stories. There the narrator muses on "the Big Guy" who now has us older folks in his sights. In Updike's scenario, as in ours, we have exited from the role of the *subject*-who-does and entered the role of the *object*-of-Someone's-gaze—we find ourselves in His sights and power. Rather than doer, we are potentially done to, found faulty, at risk of being whisked away. Think as well of old people's burgeoning entourage of doctors—an entourage that bespeaks their incapacity to "do it alone" anymore. Even their two legs—on which they used to delight in "doing it alone"—start to require the supplement of a cane.

Oedipus's capacity to think along these lines famously allowed him to solve the riddle of the Sphinx. When asked "what creature walks on four legs in the morning, two legs at noon, and three legs in the evening," only Oedipus had the insight to answer "man." For Oedipus to envisage (while on two legs as an adult) the "four legs" (two plus two arms) he once traveled on as an infant, as well as the "three legs" (two plus a cane) he will travel on late in life is a radiant insight. Yet it is blinding as well, for the riddle that yields to Oedipus's abstract thought is irresistibly reconstituted over time's passage. And reconstituted at Oedipus's expense. Decode it though he may, he cannot coordinate the trinity of different times that the riddle encompasses. No one can. Who we were, who we are, and who we will be: these are condemned to remain—despite Oedipus's conceptual grasp of all three—strangers to each other. As Marcel Proust puts it in his great novel *In Search of Lost Time*, we become ourselves only sequentially, over time *(on ne se réalise que successivement)*. We move through time in single file, so to speak—avatar by avatar. We do not cumulatively bestride it. Yet, though I can never experience childhood again, I sense that I am approaching that third leg, the time of the cane. I glimpse it coming my way.

LIGHT

I refer not to the ambient light that allows us to see, but rather the ways in which, as we age, we tend to become *light*. I am two inches shorter than I was in my sixties— and ten pounds lighter as well—but I have in mind something more than merely physical. Rather, it is the cluster of thoughts and feelings others assume about my bodily changes. *Light* in the sense of less commanding, less grounded: I have become a being with less presence. For *heavy*, consider the example of Prince Miusov, a minor figure in Fyodor Dostoevsky's *The Brothers Karamazov* who unthinkingly assumes his importance on the social scene—"a weakness," Dostoevsky writes, "forgivable in him . . . considering that he was . . . fifty years old, the age at which an intelligent and worldly man of means always becomes more respectful of himself." Obviously, in the fullness of his resources, Miusov matters!

When younger (aged fifty, say, and recognized by others as reasonably successful, tolerably well-preserved), we are more likely to "cut a figure." We are accustomed (in our own way) to making ourselves noticeable, responded to, perhaps admired, perhaps—even better—desired. But old people increasingly find themselves, so to speak, exited from the social scene before they actually leave it. They have become figures that younger people (animatedly congregating together around their shared projects and relationships) unthinkingly look away from, barely see at all. Being seen starts to morph into becoming invisible, being seen through. What we older ones choose to wear starts to lose its practical value, however we might fret over our clothes: Who is looking at us anyway?

We become *light* in other senses as well. Freed (or expelled) from arrangements that for decades grounded our familiar social identity—widowed, say—we find ourselves, in a certain sense, free-floating. Matrimony no longer means what it once did, nor does motherhood or fatherhood. Speaking of motherhood: I vividly recall my amused horror when, as a college freshman reading

Albert Camus's *The Stranger*, I came at the end to the drama of Meursault's mother. In a nursing home, nearing her own death, Mme. Meursault develops an intimate relationship with a male co-resident. At that time in my own life—I was nineteen—I could hardly imagine a more vivid instance of absurdity. At the eleventh hour, her approaching demise staring her in the face, Mme. Meursault breaks out of seemliness—and takes a lover! Lightness to the point of absurdity: the larger point of Camus's brilliant novel.

Now, much later, the scene reads otherwise, and for a couple of reasons. First, some twenty years ago my mother—in her eighties and in a nursing home—became the object of another patient's passionate attentions. She had suffered a minor stroke and was having trouble swallowing. Though her vibrancy remained intact throughout her seventies, she was now a deeply diminished woman—and hardly in search of a companion. But Mr. Moore, a co-resident at the home, had earlier dealt with the same issue of a stroke and subsequent trouble swallowing. The staff at the nursing home put them at the same table, hoping he might help her learn to swallow better. So the relationship began, and it gathered focus and intensity. Visiting my mother, I would watch Mr. Moore wheel his wheelchair into her room and come to rest next to her bed. He would take her hand, look into her eyes, and pour out his feelings. She did not reciprocate, but she did not turn him away either. "He wants to marry me," she later confided, in something close to a mangled whisper, her expression one of disbelief leavened, perhaps, by an enigmatic touch of pride. I did not know what to make of this wintry scenario, but I was old enough to grasp that it was far from absurd. To imagine that the romances of the heart that occur in nursing homes are inherently unseemly—to the point of being freakish—betrays the hasty judgment of the young(er). Older, I recognize that the heart may remain resilient, despite bodily depredations; that the capacity to fall in love—to respond to others doing so—may survive until the end.

Second, I am now in my own eighties. With age comes a certain comic self-awareness. Though we remain subjects who choose, we find ourselves—increasingly—to be pawns in a sort of game we did not ask to play and whose moves we have trouble mastering. Another power—outside our will, under the aegis of the Big Guy—is at work reshaping body and mind, reconfiguring our settings. As our literal mobility diminishes in time, other kinds of mobility—unthinkable when younger—may come into play. We glimpse the short-term-ness of arrangements that earlier felt long-term. We discover ourselves immersed in scenarios that even the most lavish life-insurance policies cannot keep at bay. Some of us may respond creatively to these alterations we never asked for.

Till death do us part: good marriages, and mine is a good one, begin by assenting to that commitment and seeking to honor it. My wife and I remain more abidingly bonded than ever, yet it is likely that one of us will die before the other: death usually *does* do us part. If this happens, the other might eventually enter a retirement community or nursing home. Given that the widowed find themselves in an altered emotional landscape, some of them engage, in time, in wintry romances—like Mr. Moore and my mother. And if they do, their offspring may respond to these eleventh-hour bondings with embarrassment, even repugnance.

Many years after my father's death (and before the short-lived advent of Mr. Moore on the scene), I vividly recall asking my mother, "Do you think very much about Daddy?" After a few moments' silence, she looked at me blankly—almost as though surprised—and her answer came: "I hardly think about him at all." I was shocked by her words. Now, nearing the age she had reached when she said them, I hear her otherwise. She may—in aging—have gradually come to lose my father as a player in her diminishing memories; twenty years is a long time. Immersed in a different environment inviting other responses, she no longer held to him as a vivid presence—which is how I, at that moment and twenty-five years younger than she, still thought of him, still needed to think of him.

I turn to *light* again, this time not as a term suggesting how the old may surprisingly re-invent themselves in their last chapters. Rather, I now refer to the drama encoded in the damaged body itself. "Fifteen apparitions have I seen," the poet Yeats writes: "the worst, a coat upon a coat-hanger." Many older people's bodies are literally becoming lighter, en route to their disappearance. How can one not notice an old friend's belt notched tighter, to hold in pants now too big, the pant-legs too long as well? How ignore the new drama of that friend's laboring (as unnoticeably as possible) to straighten his back when he slowly rises from a chair? How not look away as he carefully tends to the serious business of maintaining his balance, or the full minute it takes him to engineer his body into the back seat of the waiting taxi? He is working with an altered body in an altered setting. That work is new for him; it has its beauty and deserves respect.

A novelist once confided in me her sense of a good story's core requirement. It must change, she said, and it must do so in ways that give the earlier arrangements a new resonance. In Austen's *Pride and Prejudice*, Elizabeth Bennet's signature move from Wickham to Darcy—from error to recognition—reprises the story of maturation so beloved of Western novelists. The opposite move I have been exploring here—as one goes from solid to light—is unlikely to replace Elizabeth's recognition-moment as a novelistic staple. (How could we not prefer narratives that are pregnant with a future?) But the move from solid to light is dramatic in its own ways. Seen from the right perspective, it shines with a beauty as motley as it is somber: comic and tragic at the same time.

DE MORTUIS . . .

I have reached that age when memorial services have become an all-too-frequent occurrence. Rituals that were exotic occasions decades ago—what had such ceremonies to do with me!—have taken on a new interest. They not only reveal assumptions ripe for analysis, but the analysis itself keeps changing as I continue to age. I begin with memorial services I attended in my middle years.

Since I taught for many years at the same college, these services typically honored the death of an older colleague. What struck me at the time was a certain "mandated" falseness in the speeches being delivered. Listening to them, I would find myself awash in hyperbolic portraits of character and achievement—of dead men and women now become larger-than-life exemplars. I was being told repeatedly—each time someone rose to speak—about the dead person's remarkableness.

The Latin aphorism "De mortuis nil nisi bonum"—about the dead say nothing unless good—has been with us for a long time. Deriving from an even older Greek source, it has been recycled immemorially. We have an extensive history of speaking of the dead in this partial fashion, omitting all traits that might complicate our encomium. Indeed, who attends such ceremonial services with a desire to speak—or hear—the unvarnished truth about the one who has recently died? Nevertheless, the saccharine flavor of these testimonials eventually left me feeling cheated—all the more if I knew the person well. I had trouble recognizing my old friend in the wealth of superlatives covering him over, obscuring the traits I remembered best. My sense of community compelled me to attend these services, but increasingly I came to believe that the language deployed in them was—inevitably and for good reasons—meretricious. It was not serious language, not the truth of the departed figure. For me at that time, memorial services were essentially about the one who had died.

Some fifteen years ago, however, I started to experience these ceremonies differently. The language deployed in them had not changed, but my relation to the purpose behind the words had altered. Nearer to death myself, I began to hear the encomia otherwise—still not as accurate portraits of the deceased, but now as heartfelt testimonials from those left behind and expressing their grief. My takeaway from these ceremonies likewise changed. I now began to feel that I had missed something important. I had been in the dead person's presence for years—yet without paying adequate attention, without taking the measure. I had been asleep at the post—and had lost someone whose preciousness I failed to appreciate while that person was alive. Others were showing me, all unintentionally, how much I had overlooked.

Now in my eighties, I have arrived at yet another perspective on memorial services. "De mortuis nil nisi bonum" may be less about those who have just died than about the living who will in their own time die as well. The generosity invoked by the aphorism, I now see, resembles that of the Sermon on the Mount. Speak of the dead, now, as you would have others speak of you dead, later. A good deal nearer to my own memorial (should there be one) than I was fifteen years ago, I recognize more of death's shaping sway over this phenomenon—death serving to inspire a certain strange beauty.

I now grasp that the founding reality of all memorial services is a gaping absence where once there was presence. The dead are gone; their absence is both irreparable and generative. Left with our love for one who has departed, we make speeches that deliver not the lineaments of the absent one but the contours of what we now realize we have lost—contours that death has made luminous. Thomas Hardy's greatest love poetry centers on his dead wife Emma, as in "The Voice":

> Woman much missed, how you call to me, call to me,
> Saying that now you are not as you were
> When you had changed from the one who was all to me,
> But as at first, when our day was fair.

Can it be you that I hear? Let me view you, then,
Standing as when I drew near to the town
Where you would wait for me: yes, as I knew you then,
Even to the original air-blue gown!

While alive, Emma complicated Hardy's life in countless ways; it was not an easy marriage. But once dead, she begins to serve, inexhaustibly, as his muse. He now possesses in full, an unbearably precious picture of what he has lost. Dead and in the grave, Emma calls out to him as she had not for years, and his imagination goes on to recover the enchantment of their early courtship, "even to the original air-blue gown!"

In ways that we do not enjoy admitting, our commerce with the dead may be easier than our commerce with the living. It is at any rate *different*. They can no longer push back, counter or correct our thoughts and feelings. Insofar as our dead still live, they do so within our hearts and minds. Our love brings them back to life—this time on our terms. I do not want to be uncharitable, but I believe that Hardy now had his Emma where he could do the most with her. Now that she was no longer there, he could wholeheartedly articulate his love, free from interruption.

Hardy's is a famous example, but the phenomenon happens daily and to the humblest of us. One of my good friends lost his wife some while ago, and—a few months after her death—he told me that the love he was experiencing for her now was more intense than anything he had felt while she was still alive. Her look, her way of walking and talking, her throwaway gestures: these now lodged achingly inside him. Though he could no longer touch her or talk to her, he was "realizing" her as never before. Her intensity would in time fade—abstractly he knew this—but right now she was an absence that filled him up. In the memorial service he later organized for his dead wife—several months after her death—many spoke of what she had meant for them. But none so movingly and extensively as my friend, the grieving husband.

As I reflect on it, his painful-to-witness act of witnessing seemed shaped to several purposes. On the one hand, it articulated—in naked, emotionally wrought language—what others in that room were feeling at a less intense level. No less, it attempted to express—and thus in part assuage—the guilt he could not escape feeling for having outlived her. (Such guilt is no less intense for being baseless.) Finally, it gave him his chance to say in public, for the only time in his life, everything that he felt toward the wife he had lost, the countless ways in which she had made his life possible. Need I say that these are ultimate declarations he could not earlier have summoned into utterance? As memorial services keep revealing, the absence imposed by death is a creative player in the social dramas underway.

Perhaps we can go further. Does it take death to enable our fullest love-portrait of someone else? Do the dimensions of a cherished partner become unbearably dear, only after we've lost the partner? In his essay "The Storyteller," the critic Walter Benjamin cites another writer's claim that "a man who dies at the age of thirty-five is at every point of his life a man who dies at the age of thirty-five." Then Benjamin adds: "Nothing is more dubious than this sentence—but for the sole reason that the tense is wrong. A man . . . who died at thirty-five will appear to *remembrance* at every point in his life as a man who dies at the age of thirty-five." *Memory*, the living who are now remembering the dead: that is the source of the energy giving the belated portrait its narrative wholeness in time, its overpowering cogency. What are memorial services but arenas in which the shaping power of memory allows the bereft to delineate what now appears to be the *whole* person who has departed? Given the resonance of their newly bestowed finality, is it any wonder they seem larger than life? Benjamin reveals what I could not see before: that our grief-charged language, as we remember the dead, invests them with a beauty whose dimensions we could not have accessed or articulated while they were alive. As though what was earlier black and white has been sprung by death into unforgettable color.

The implications of the foregoing claims are sobering. Could it be that we grasp the fullest sense of another being only in the wake of that other's absence? That it takes their material absence to fund our deepest feelings for them? Proust's *In Search of Lost Time* is steeped in this conviction and takes it all the way. His protagonist, Marcel, loves a woman, Albertine, only so long as he cannot possess her and make her his own. Inexorably, his passion leads him to sequester her in his home—this part of the novel is entitled *The Prisoner*—and no less inexorably, her ongoing presence does not cease to bore him. One of the strangest scenes in the novel reveals his solution to this dilemma. He makes a ritual of observing her, with hypnotic intensity, as she lies asleep on his bed—wonderfully absent now (she is unconscious after all), yet deliciously present too (her quiescent body no longer resisting). I do not wish to take the point as far as Proust does—that only the absence of those we love allows us to grasp the depth of our love for them. But I do claim that absence—whether death-caused or occurring otherwise—is generative in ways we rarely reckon. From it may come scenarios suffused with strange beauty.

Let me close this set of reflections by bringing it up to date and changing the analysis yet again. My wife and I recently attended a memorial service for her cousin Robbie. He had succumbed a few months earlier, after years of resistance, to an incurable cancer. I was hesitant to attend the service. I wondered if propriety and "manners" might paper over the loss that, in their different ways, everyone was grieving. What took place, instead, was a set of surprises I had not anticipated.

I had known Robbie for much of my life (at a certain distance, not as his siblings or cousins knew him). His sisters, his in-laws, and his friends all spoke movingly of him. As they spoke, the various absence-logics I've been describing above still applied. These were portraits enabled by death, given their point and poignance by Robbie's disappearance. Yet I found myself shocked by their immediate emotional power. I felt I was now seeing the "extensions" of Robbie himself—how he continued to live inside those who loved him—uncannily brought back to life. Brought back less as rounded, wide-angled summaries than as vivid, zoom-takes on Robbie's "quick," his quirky vividness. The ceremony made me realize that, though *absence* lets you grasp a fullness that presence invariably lacks, *presence* may assault you with a power that absence cannot match. To be immersed in the ongoing present reality of others together—grieving, sharing, talking, joking—this was exactly what I had *not* imagined the service would entail. Its emotional intensity put to shame the abstract notions I had framed in advance.

Robbie's memorial service as a shared present experience—that does not invalidate the other absence-shaped memorial models I have tried to sketch. But it claims its place in the sequence, inasmuch as it signals that the generative dimension of all memorial models is time itself. Whether it be past times we have lived through and are now reseeing, differently, or a present experience we are powerfully moved by, time is the shape-shifting premise that sets and resets the scene. And more: only time as presence allows living others into our space, where their co-presence can affect us in startling ways. However intricately we may revisit and remap past experiences, it takes a moment of shared presence to suddenly move us—and take us where we didn't dream we'd go.

POSTMORTEM

Who does not lament the lessening and loss of bodily generativity? As Yeats confronted the mounting evidence of his physical decline, he sought ever more strenuously to imagine another way of being. He came to envisage the task of old age as an imaginative departure from the sensuous settings of youth—the "young in one another's arms," "the mackerel-crowded seas." Those realms of lovemaking and spawning were "no country for old men." In their place he urged a creative journey to another kind of setting altogether—a reconfigured vision of ancient Byzantium. Once we arrive there, metaphorically, our focus will shift from bodily diminishment to the pursuit of transcendent values—those lodged in "monuments of unageing intellect." Mind triumphantly over matter.

I have argued above for the beauty and interest of aging in terms considerably less sublime, more pedestrian, than

Yeats's "Sailing to Byzantium." Generativity need not be envisaged within his rigidly oppositional terms: either bodily fecundity or monuments of intellect, nothing in between. Rather, generativity might flourish in in-between scenarios—as a variable, close-to-the-ground resource we carry within us, virtually to the grave itself. Its true measure goes beyond testosterone and estrogen levels, on the one hand, or sublime works of art and thought, on the other. It flickers in the body long past our days of spawning; it is alive in retirement communities and nursing homes as well. Hardy's poems devoted to his dead wife draw on postmortem inspiration, but so—in more modest ways—do those memorials for the dead that loom larger year after year. Is it any wonder, finally, that death—the worst thing most of us can imagine—brings forth an infinite range of responses large and small? Even as death marks our inescapable creatureliness, it fuels creative departures. If it is a commonplace that we do not know what to do with death, it is no less true that we would not know what to do without it.

LESS

ess became an unavoidable horizon during the initial onslaught of COVID in early 2020. Whatever our age, the plague we began to suffer from carried the ambient threat of either *less* life (sudden onset of illness, with who knows what consequences) or *no* life (our life not just upended, but ended). This general picture came to resemble, suddenly, the more benign version that retirees have long struggled to live with: a life marked by less. Indeed, the elderly have earned their right to view with irony the foundational premise of the American dream itself—*more* and *better*.

Unlike all other nations, America is founded on more and better. Over four hundred years ago, the Puritans came to these shores wanting more room and better conditions to thrive than their home-countries permitted. For two and a half centuries, the siren call of Jefferson's Declaration of Independence—life, liberty, and the pursuit of happiness—has exerted an irresistible appeal. These days, of course—and not least because of COVID—there is a growing fear that, on the political front, this dream may be played out. Yet even so, our American expectation of more and better to come—our assumption of it as virtually a birthright—feels so deeply rooted as to be beyond relinquishing.

Against the grain of these assumptions, what does life look like, seen through the lens of less? I concede at the outset that no one under seventy is likely to make this case. Yet the conditions I explore are no unique province of the aged. Each period of life suffers/enjoys its particular emphases; each has its "you'd have to be there" aspect. I take this "you'd have to be there" aspect to signal a sort of three-dimensional vividness that only events experienced in the present possess. Those at a distance from us (either younger or older) tend to register such events otherwise, by way of invariably reductive scenarios. The felt vividness bestowed by *now* disappears into the flatness of anticipation or memory. I focus here on experiences that anyone might have, but that the elderly are likely to register with three-dimensional intensity—as burden, but also as gift.

LESS (A)SLEEP: 3 A.M.

It is virtually a truism that older people tend to sleep less and that the sleep they get is more fitful, interrupted by bouts of waking. For me personally, the most upsetting of these bouts—the hardest to get past—tend to arrive around 3 a.m. At this hour, moves and assumptions that felt unproblematic during the day—that had been clean forgotten by dinnertime!—may reemerge within the mind, laden now with menace.

Why might events that seemed untroubling when they occurred at 3 p.m. become problematic when revisited twelve hours later? I suggest that it is not the behavior that has suddenly revealed its unsettling charge but, rather, it is we—unfortunately awake at that ungodly hour—who have lost our resourcefulness. Our diminished capacity—at 3 a.m.—to patrol our thoughts and feelings seems impishly to energize those same thoughts and feelings. Is it our becoming passive prey that turns them into active hunters, hunting us? Why might this happen often enough to be a syndrome in need of interpretation?

There is, first, the literal darkness of 3 a.m. Do we ever grasp the extent to which visually recognizing objects and others bolsters (all day long) our familiar sense of ourselves? If identity itself is a corroborative premise—no "me" there without a "you" to confirm it—this model of corroboration falters in the middle of the night. Others have exited from our world. Even that partner bodily in our bed is essentially elsewhere, unconscious. The mere presence of another familiar body may alleviate our isolation, but that is not the same as two awake people confirming each other in a shared space.

Next, defenses we draw on unceasingly to massage our daily experience so that it meshes with our self-image—these seem to have gone AWOL at 3 a.m. (They will return when we awaken in the morning, but we need them now.) By defenses, I have in mind a sort of protective apparatus installed at the heart of my thinking processes. This apparatus seems responsible for the flow of self-justifying thoughts that accompany me throughout the day. Though no evidence of such an apparatus exists, I have no trouble identifying how it operates. Here are some instances. If the car behind me this afternoon honked at me as it passed, that is because its driver was in a hurry and impatient—not because I made a right turn (the turnoff came up fast) without, perhaps, having given my turn signal. If the TV crime serial we watched last night left me frustrated, that's because its character motivations weren't well developed—not because I'm having trouble keeping up with the visual and verbal logic of TV dramas as I get older. If my brother and his wife voted for Trump in 2016, and again in 2020 and 2024, that's because they're selfishly protecting their wealth—not because cogent reasons may exist for doubting that the Democrats would get the job done. You get the drift. I needn't go into heavier matters that emerge when my defenses start to fail—like why did I retire when I did? Do we have enough money to sustain our old age? Which of us will die first?

The upshot is that we elderly who get less sleep are losing something of the self-justifying fabric of thoughts and feelings that used to serve us well. Our identity— insofar as it may be thought of as a fortress—is less adept at resisting life's various micro-assaults; at 3 a.m. we do not cope so well. Put otherwise, our actual relation to our world—that relation seen from a perspective no longer massaged for our approval—comes more into view. When it does, we may not like what we see. One reason older people may be less content than younger ones is that we are at risk of recognizing more of who we really are than is good for us. That is a nocturnal development we'd prefer less of. Yet—for exactly these reasons—the 3 a.m. perspective is a potential gift. It might even be a wake-up call.

LESS (A)SLEEP: AWAKENING

I have never forgotten a minor event that occurred nearly forty years ago. I was teaching at Swarthmore College then, and my sixteen-year-old daughter had just gotten her driver's license. It was now legal for her, late that afternoon (school had ended an hour earlier), to drive our second car. With her best friend beside her in the front seat, she was following my wife in our other car. They were going shopping or to some nearby event—I don't remember what. While they were out, I was at home in my study, preparing the next day's classes. Up till then it was—as Arnold Bennett says of June 16, 1904, in Joyce's *Ulysses*—"the dailiest day possible."

The phone rang at 4 p.m., and since I was alone in the house, I answered it (reluctantly: I was deep into setting up my classes). An unfamiliar female voice said, "Are you the owner of a green 1985 Toyota with this license plate?" It was indeed our plate, our car. She then said, "Don't worry, a policeman is on the scene, your daughter is all right," and hurried off the phone.

Panic overtook me. A moment earlier I was revising my notes for a novella by Joseph Conrad (*Heart of Darkness*: I knew it almost by heart). Now my life had suddenly slipped out of my control, come undone. What had happened to my daughter? Where was my wife? My life was out of control in another sense too: its meaning was no longer inside me but outside, in a setting I knew nothing of, in thrall to a violence as undeniable as it was unknown. These were pre-cell-phone days, so it took a few more minutes for my wife to reach me (going into a neighbor's house, borrowing the neighbor's phone).

What had just happened, my wife explained, was that she had driven across a busy intersection (not far from our house), and our daughter in the second car—seeing her mother go across—had immediately followed her. (It was as though she didn't want to lose sight of her mother.) She had not noticed the car speedily approaching after my wife got across, however, and the two cars collided. The front right fender of our car was shattered, and my daughter's friend (in the "suicide seat") was a few inches away from a bodily harm you didn't want to think about. Both girls were terrified, but neither was hurt; nor was the driver of the other car.

Technically it was true, what the unknown caller (the driver of the other car) had told me: my daughter had not been hurt. But the psychological drama went otherwise. Rather than being soothed by her telling me my daughter was unharmed, those words released—like a genie sprung from the bottle—the entire accident in its worst guise. I helplessly replayed it, second by second—saw her mangled body—and then remembered that, actually, no one had been hurt. There would be repair costs to pay, but—all cooler heads would agree—we had been lucky that day. That bullet we imagine with our name on it had hit home, but it had been a blank.

The good news notwithstanding, I was immersed in a sea of aftershock. I could not stop replaying what might have happened, could not put to rest what had been borne in on me: that my daughter was mortal. That's when I grasped that I normally live at half speed (at best), as most of us do, enclosed in a torpor of self-protec-tive assumptions. I believe—almost all the time—that I am safe: it won't happen to me. "The quickest of us walk about well wadded with stupidity," George Eliot writes in *Middlemarch*. Our ego-defenses are our "stupid-ity"—Oedipus wasn't especially worried before Tiresias arrived—yet, if we were less "well wadded," would our lives still feel like they were assuredly *ours*?

Another related vignette: one of my older colleagues had served in World War II, and he often tried to explain to me the psychic cost exacted by his wartime experience. His outfit had been assigned to the eastern part of France those awful months in late 1944, pursuing the Germans as they slowly retreated. He found it impossible—day after day—to keep from knowing that he might be killed. He ended up gravely wounded instead—for which he was awarded the Purple Heart—but what I call the "aftershock" rarely left him thereafter. He had experienced for too long that it could happen to him tomorrow; he could not "unknow" what he knew. You cannot be in the presence of death that long, he would tell me over the years, and not be changed by it.

I take this extensive detour through my daughter's minor accident and my colleague's traumatic war experience to claim the following. The elderly have more difficulty ignoring what is in store for them: the primordial "less" that they feel menaced by is less life itself. The still-intact "stupidity" of the young is no longer the birthright of the elderly. Is it any surprise that the latter may sleep less—that those 3 a.m. moments insist on visitation privileges? But is it possible that such unwelcome moments might constitute genuine awakenings? That it is valuable to recognize one's life in all its unmassaged unprotectedness, its vulnerability to invasive change? That what George Eliot calls "stupidity" might really be stupidity, even if our sanity, survival, and health depend on retaining a precious measure of it? I shall sound this theme again—stupidity or awakening?—as I turn to health: another birthright that the elderly enjoy less of.

LESS HEALTH

The body's lessening health awakens in the mind a kind of awareness—and appreciation—that the robust rarely think about. Some things you grasp most keenly, it may be, only when something about them starts to go wrong, when the "wadding" starts to fail. Elderly people's bodies—sooner or later—go wrong; they are programmed to do so. A few years ago, I had an encounter with a new doctor that sheds light on this phenomenon.

Since he was replacing my old doctor, a certain amount of paperwork needed to be filled out before I could meet with him. This included a brief psychological profile—a couple of dozen standard questions you answer on a scale of one to five (one indicating serene bliss, five conveying impenetrable depression). Sitting in the reception room, I made the mistake of responding candidly—mainly threes, with the odd two or four, but no ones or fives. Twenty minutes later he showed up and introduced himself. Along with his handshake came these words: "Well, you're pretty obsessive-compulsive, aren't you?" I was shocked (the mistake I alluded to above is that most patients fudge their answers toward the bright side). I pushed back against his leaping to conclusions—he had never met me before—even as, silently, reluctantly, I recognized a smidgeon of truth in his charge.

He was willing to keep his mind open, he said, so I expanded on my "answers" by providing further detail about my life. He listened attentively for a few minutes, then shifted to a different diagnosis. My problem, he now informed me, is that I "overthink" things. At this I really did bridle. Something essential about how I understand life itself was being demeaned by a man who had known me less than ten minutes. I labored to get him to understand how and why "overthinking" has served as the gold standard of my professional life. I was on the verge of trotting out Socrates's memorable saying a couple of millennia ago—"The unexamined life is not worth living"—but common sense prevailed. I merely said that, as a professor of the humanities, I'd done my best to practice "overthinking." The hallmark of serious thinking is to call into question one's earlier thinking—to remain on guard against self-deception. (Self-deceivers—as far as professorial values go—belong in Dante's lowest circle in hell.) "Overthinking," I ended up claiming, is how we come closest to the impersonal truth of things: how they are, independent of our preferences.

The doctor was unimpressed. "It's bad for your health," he insisted. "Your blood pressure and major organs, your state of mind and state of nerves: all of these suffer from overthinking. Keep on doing it—you're seventy-eight after all—and it could kill you," he said. This left me in a quandary I had never confronted before. What he peremptorily dismissed as "overthinking" had contributed, I knew, to my best writing and teaching. Yet I was now seventy-eight (he had that right), and it was true that I was seeing him because my blood pressure—always high—had been going higher for the past couple of years. I left his office baffled. Could his judgment be right—less for who I used to be than for who I had become?

Musing further on it, I'm unable to say who was right— unable as well to split the difference between us. For I have devoted my life to overthinking. Inasmuch as our defenses continuously distort the world in our favor, our only hope of seeing things as they really are requires that we labor to get our subconscious biases out of the way. Over time, a tidy professional career has rewarded these attempts. Dig deeper/think further/come upon the unknown of what you were sure you knew: That has been a sort of credo. Could it now be a death warrant?

Aging exposes the body to stresses that only get worse. Persevering in a sustained way against the grain of shared commonplaces takes effort—effort that (as in prolonged swimming against the tide) may in time exact its toll. Could making peace with the given—with the current of things as they appear—mean something more than lazy-mindedness? Might this, as a stance, be wiser than ever-watchful suspicion?

In sum, protracted "overthinking" may not merely damage an old man's health. It may keep him from accepting at face value the bounty of what is daily given—what is right before his eyes. Whether it be a moment of intimacy or responding to the radiance of a sunset, the elderly need to find ways of saying yes to precious things on offer, now. Being in the moment: that is what that doctor was recommending, just as it is what a great tennis player exhibits when playing each point for all it is worth, each point one at a time. Zoom or wide angle: I have lived my professional life in the service of the wide angle, bringing the hitherto distant and unseen to bear on the picture before me. But perhaps there is wisdom in the zoom perspective. Play this thing we call life moment by moment—as the tennis champion plays the game he's immersed in, not the match he'll come to next if he wins this one. In any case the game will eventually reach its end: Best to enjoy the experience of getting there.

LESS DISTRACTION: TIME FOR RECKONING

Travel is perhaps the favorite form of distraction to which retirees are drawn. Gigantic cruise ships—floating cities of the elderly—traverse the globe, promising their clientele authentic encounters with exotica. These promises are largely fraudulent. Genuine engagement with other cultures requires more than brief lectures, PowerPoint presentations, and colorful films. Zodiac tours may take us to where aborigines live, but merely getting there cannot pass on to us their aboriginal culture. Which may be fine: many of the elderly have limited energies, and they never signed on for the conceptual labor required for deeper encounters. Their problem is elsewhere. In 2020 and 2021 cruise ship travel more or less ground to a global halt, thanks to the COVID pandemic.

With the curtailment of travel, options for elderly distraction diminish. It becomes harder to avoid the self-reckoning that less work, less sleep, less health, and now less travel bring in their tow. No one has put this better than T. S. Eliot in *Four Quartets*:

> And last, the rending pain of re-enactment
> Of all that you have done, and been; the shame
> Of motives late revealed, and the awareness
> Of things ill done and done to others' harm
> Which once you took for exercise of virtue.
> Then fools' approval stings, and honour stains.

Eliot articulates, exquisitely, the drama of defenses crumbling, of our later recognizing self-interested moves that had earlier, cunningly, passed themselves off as "exercise of virtue." Even honorary degrees—the North Star of the most successful of the elderly—cannot protect against that sting, that stain.

I have devoted my life to literary reckoning. At Harvard for years and at Swarthmore for decades, I saw my task as the reckoning of literary values, as teaching students how to recognize and assess those values. I have tried to help others see what was most resonantly at play in the verbal patterning of a poem, a play, or a novel. I understood my job as a staging of encounters between the minds of readers and the exquisitely crafted humanity of texts. The realm of sublime literary achievements: That was the garden I was privileged to spend my time laboring in.

So it is an unwelcome insight to see something of myself in Eliot's lines, to recognize that not only are there snakes in this garden, but that I—the gardener—have brought some of them in. The activities of writing and teaching literature—like all human activities—are saturated in ego-energies. We bring ourselves (our strengths but no less our limitations) into our work. However obscurely, we are always arguing the brief of ourselves. Fueled by creaturely shortcomings, my critical acumen has battened on a self-evading critique focused on others. A life spent in reckoning with works of art has, all adroitly, spared me from a good deal of self-reckoning. Now retired, I tend to find myself less spared—especially at 3 a.m.

LESS AND MORE

I have already quoted Yeats's haunting lines—"Fifteen apparitions have I seen: The worst, a coat upon a coat-hanger"—and it should come as no surprise that Yeats wrote them late in life. To glimpse the signs of one's slowly disappearing body is literally to see some of our bodily "wadding" wasted away, and to understand, anew, the lifelong desire for more. Who doesn't want more? Life, liberty, and happiness: Does anyone ever have enough of these? America is founded on the wistful gap between things as they stubbornly are and things as we want them to be—a gap that cannot be closed.

I claimed at the outset that the conditions I explore are no unique province of the aged. Let me close by proposing that—though we don't like to think about this—*less* operates, throughout our lives, as a dimension of our creaturely DNA, underwriting the systolic-diastolic rhythms of our living in time. To consider this claim, think for a moment about famous people you know of and their fabulous adventures—their love affairs, their tumultuous time in the limelight, their famous friends, their remarkable achievements and notable failures.

Against such extravagant fullness, how could I not concede the penury of my life? My scorecard is diminutive—all but invisible compared to the magnitude of theirs. One wife, two children, no affairs, a single profession, a number of books written (no bestsellers among them), my share of unfulfilled hopes and lingering regrets (none of these in the public domain). The famous folks' *more* dwarfs my meager *less*.

But in the light shed by Yeats's coat upon a coat-hanger—the light of our passing—to what extent does anyone *continue to possess* the *more* that their scorecard indicates as theirs? Our passage through time makes us all leaky creatures, incapable of holding onto our experience. Ask Clinton or Bush or Obama how much their time in the White House shapes their current grasp of what their lives mean to them. Ask an aging Casanova how much his earlier affairs play into his present sense of himself. *Less* stubbornly marks our common lot. We are condemned—perhaps blessed as well—to be the being that gains and loses being as we move through time. If *less* were not wrought into the very fabric of our identity, we would not, incorrigibly, keep dreaming of *more*.

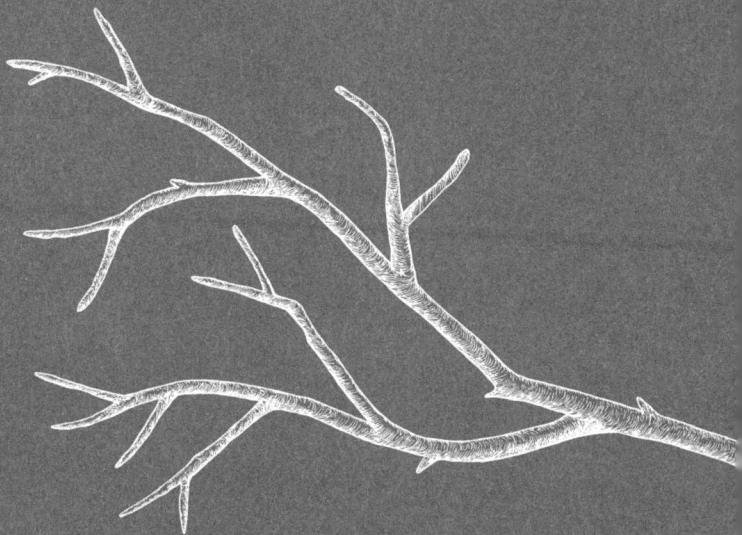

DORMANCY

A long time ago my twin brother and I went away to the same college. For the next four years we were intensively lectured to, by professors sometimes so gifted that he and I still remember vividly the best of them: their learning and passion, their craft, their gestures and their exact way with words. After graduation I used to return now and then for reunions—my brother rarely— but that part of our past seemed increasingly behind us. Probably dead. Or was it merely dormant? In 2021 our class officers proposed to launch a program of lectures that differed significantly from those we had once listened to. The officers would invite members of our class—ones who, over the years, had developed various expertises—to give lectures (via Zoom) to our classmates. This time we would be both the lecturers and the "lecturees."

I gave such a talk in 2021, but I want to focus on my twin brother's talk, delivered three years later. (We had both become college professors of literature, hence been invited to say our say.) My own talk has become blurred in my mind over time, but my brother's remains strangely alive. My being personally uninvolved probably heightened my alertness to the drama of his speaking to our class. Indeed, three dimensions of his talk struck me as simply begging to be further unpacked: first, what we all *looked* like (this was a Zoom lecture), second, what exactly he was claiming, and third, what it meant, more broadly, for us "lecturees" to have become lecturers. (If the referent in my subsequent remarks remains male, that is because the college we attended was all male at that time. Happily, within a decade of our graduation, the college went co-ed. Twenty-seven years after my graduation, our older daughter would graduate from there as well.)

To begin with how we looked: Well, we looked awful— that is, everyone except for me. I hasten to clarify that remark: I didn't look as bad as they did only because I cannot *see* the age that is written on my face. None of us can see our own age. But we sure can see that of others (it is something we become good at as we get older). I do not doubt that, for those classmates on the Zoom talk looking at me, I appeared just as decrepit, heading grave-ward, as they did to me.

My brother's talk focused on William Faulkner's *Go Down, Moses*—a novel I shall have more to say about—and he dwelled on its difficulty for first-time readers. To describe how that text might now—many decades later—have taken on resonance, he used the term "dormant." Faulkner's novel, he suggested, was dormant in us—a dormancy ready to waken as soon as we were ready to grasp its "sleeping" contents. As soon as we became self-reflective enough to see what was all along at stake in it.

Staring at these aged faces on the screen, and especially at those I had known fairly well, I kept catching sight—all but hypnotically—of their vibrant young faces of sixty-five years ago, the faces before the faces they now wore. Oddly, the differences were as apt as they were appalling: those wintry faces were unmistakable remakes of the springtime faces that had once been theirs. The old faces, if you could make yourself not look away, lay dormant in the younger ones of those I had known and cared for. Each of these old men was, as regards himself, solidly installed in his present incarnation, undisturbed by what he looked like. It was I who experienced double vision, glimpsing a *then* that had been uncannily replaced by a *now*. I have long appreciated Robert Burns's memorable lines (written over two hundred years ago), "O wad some Pow'r the giftie gie us / To see oursels as ithers see us." But surely single vision is no less a gift. Could we bear to see the change in ourselves that shocks us when we see it in others?

Many great writers have dealt with these time-realities, none more powerfully than Marcel Proust. Perhaps the most haunting scene in his huge novel, *In Search of Lost Time*, occurs near the end: at the Prince de Guermantes's afternoon party. After many years spent in a sanatorium trying to regain his health, the narrator (named Marcel) attends that party. He had been intimately familiar with the Guermantes circle during his younger years, but he is now shocked by what he is seeing: "For a few seconds I did not understand why it was that I had difficulty in recognizing the master of the house and his guests and why everyone in the room appeared to have put on a disguise—in most cases a powdered wig—which changed him completely." Why are the men all wearing powdered wigs? What has happened to their hair? Coming upon one of his former acquaintances, Argencourt—now grown old—Marcel is confounded: "Disguise, carried to this extent, ceases to be a mere art, it becomes a total trans-formation of the personality. And indeed, although certain details assured me that it was really Argencourt who presented this ludicrous and picturesque spectacle, I had to traverse an almost infinite number of successive states of a single face if I wished to rediscover that of the Argencourt whom I had known and who was now, though he had no other materials than his own body with which to effect the change, so different from himself." Inexorably, this outward drama makes its way inward, into Marcel himself. Eventually, after seeing his oldest acquaintance, Bloch, at the party, looking inexplicably different from the young man Marcel used to know, as well as after hearing swatches of nearby conversations referring to himself, Marcel, as an older man, it suddenly dawns: "Then I understood that this was because he [Bloch] was in fact old and that adolescents who survive for a sufficient number of years are the material out of which life makes old men."

Adolescents who survive long enough . . . become old men. There is no middle ground of maturity. We remain young, young, young—until we realize one day that we are old. How did this happen? We never saw it coming. When it finally registers (if it ever does), it is as a fait accompli. Speechlessly, inexplicably, our age has finally found and claimed us, yet even then a part of us does not believe it. I still see my oldest childhood friend as a kid, even though he walks with a cane and is managing incurable prostate cancer. I think of my eighty-four-year-old self as a boy still. That sobriquet has been wildly inappropriate for decades, but it corresponds to the coloration of my inner landscape. When a male friend joins me for lunch and we order a glass or two of wine with our meal, I see it as a boys' outing—just a step away from "playing hooky" from our spouses. My ailments (and I will come to one of them in time) are those of old men, but they feel like encumberments arbitrarily imposed on someone still young.

DORMANCY: BODY DRAMAS

Dormancy's primary meanings refer to biological processes: how plants and animals manage on a regulated basis to hibernate so as to reduce their expenditure of energy and extend their lives. Such dormancy is benign—a biological process designed to increase the organism's longevity.

In opposition to this is the malignant dormancy we speak of when someone's earlier cancer—long thought vanquished—reappears in the body, its menace intact again. *Hibernating*—in this context—seems like a ruse carried out over time, maybe a long time, but only for a time. The returning disorder is more frightening now since it has withstood previous treatment and seems intent on destroying its host. Now it seems personal—more like the return of the repressed or a secret sharer—as though its bond with its victim were immune to time's passage, and it will have its way.

Dormancy operates on both the physiological and the psychological planes. One thinks of earlier forms of trauma that seemed overcome but that, decades later, may reclaim the mind again, their virulence untamed. It seems less that they went away on their own than that, by way of counseling or drugs or subsequent experiences, they were temporarily put to sleep. For a while, until now.

One of my college classmates—who lived on Martha's Vineyard as I do and had become a good friend—died a few months before he could watch my brother's Zoom lecture. He was probably a victim of "dormancy," though it took years to establish the likely causality of his eventually fatal Parkinson's disease. I had known him slightly when we were both undergraduates, and it was a joy to rediscover him on the Vineyard. A strapping young man back in college, he had become a passionate outdoorsman: hiking, camping, white-water rafting, kayaking, sailing. But he had also done his stint with the Marine Corps in the 1960s and drunk the waters of Camp Lejeune. Forty years later, Parkinson's symptoms began to emerge. Minor difficulties of walking and standing and bodily coordination gradually became major and then got worse. You could see he was headed toward the wheelchair. All along he kept up his courage, sustained his wit. The last time I saw him—at a dinner party—I marveled at his capacity to enter and direct the conversation around the table. He managed this from the most distorted of postures, his head lowered a foot and a half below those of the others, but his face turned upward, his eyes engaging the rest of us, his mind intact, his voice his own. Is this another dimension of dormancy and awakening—the disease that, long asleep, wakens, reveals itself, and does its damage; but no less, the mind and will, likewise awakened to the menace, and determined to resist?

Some months ago I learned that my closest colleague at the college where I taught for over forty years had become desperately ill. Younger than I, more athletic too, he had gotten clear of a bad marriage and recently remarried, this time happily. His latest book had come out to great reviews, his students (as ever) loved his courses, he was in a good place for the last chapters of his professional life. Then—having recently become an aficionado of pickleball—he started to have trouble picking up the ball. Two months later, he was seized by unbearable back pain. He rushed to his doctor who, after one long look at him sprawled out on the table, sent him to the emergency room of a nearby hospital. Soon enough the diagnosis emerged: He had advanced multiple myeloma. More, a tumor the size of his palm was growing in his back, had already cracked one of his vertebral walls, and was near to rupturing the spinal cord and paralyzing him.

No one knows the cause of multiple myeloma, nor is there a cure. (The Mayo Clinic concludes its brief online description of the disease with these oddly touching sentences: "There's no way to prevent multiple myeloma. If you get multiple myeloma, you didn't do anything to cause it.") But it occurs most often in men in their late sixties (my friend's age), and Mayo points out that a family history of multiple myeloma increases the risk of getting the disease. If one asks if dormancy is operative here, the frustrating answer seems to be—maybe. The disease's prehistory is an enigma. Something awful is happening inside him—it is his with a vengeance—but no knows how or why it found him.

One last instance, this one my own, and mercifully less urgent. I have undergone one surgical operation in my life—a laminectomy whose looming prospect long terrified me. I nevertheless chose to do it, eleven years ago, because I was suffering from severe lower back pain that would not yield to lesser forms of treatment. I was by then in my early seventies and for the past decade had faithfully carried out every set of exercises remotely likely to ease my pain. I had twice taken cortisone injections (for a brief time, effective); I had tried acupuncture; I had even consented to wear (for a month) a specially designed thick belt tight around my middle that was supposed to keep me properly "aligned." Nothing helped. So I took a deep breath and said yes to the surgery.

That's an older man's front story: an operation successfully addressing three conditions that the elderly often suffer from: scoliosis, stenosis, and arthritis. The back story is the story of how these three conditions located me as their field of operations. Two of them, indeed—arthritis and stenosis—are common enough in the elderly, but scoliosis, curvature of the spine? When and why did that arrive? To try to answer this, I have scrutinized my past, looking for clues. And one has emerged in memory—notable even back then, but infrared now. Thirty-eight years before the operation, I was a young college professor on my first sabbatical leave, in southwestern France. My wife and I were in the car a lot, I did the driving, and my back was giving me constant pain. When I finally saw a doctor, he was at a loss to understand why I hurt so much. But as I was leaving his office (still clueless), he suddenly told me to stop—and then take ten steps—and then stop again. Watching me do this, he came to his analysis (I'll never forget his French phrasing): "Mais vous avez un problème statique!" Roughly translated: "You have a problem standing up straight!" Hearing this but hardly understanding its import, I stood there, motionless, as he walked behind me, took some measurements, and went on to explain that one of my legs was notably shorter than the other. That therefore I didn't quite stand up straight. That, many years earlier, my spine had had to compensate for this misalignment. That it did so by curving back toward the longer leg, so as to make my posture more nearly vertical. This all happened long ago, he surmised. Spinal scoliosis typically follows from an uneven growth spurt in the early teens, after one leg has failed to match the growth spurt of the other.

Pursuing this further, I now see that my "problem standing up straight" reveals dormancy as a mind dynamic no less than a body dynamic. For I had, after all, been *looking at* my body in the mirror, seeing one hip slightly lower than the other, virtually every day of my life. Seeing it but not *seeing* it, for as long as I can remember. Until it first became legible at thirty-four—but fully interpretable only now, at eighty-four.

The scoliosis that served dormantly as a "correction"—for decades—eventually awakened, so to speak, and began to make trouble on its own. There followed (throughout my forties and fifties) a comedy of varying shoe inserts for the foot of the shorter leg, to equalize the leg lengths. I never did find one that worked for me, and eventually I determined to accept the back and legs I have. This worked well, sort of, for many more years, until it didn't. Eventually I went under the knife. Thanks to that laminectomy, I am still walking, as free of pain as I am likely to be: more or less the way many eighty-four-year-olds walk.

The larger point of these mini-narratives is clear. As we reach old age, our bodies—and our minds so dependent on them—are wearing out the coping strategies that earlier worked. As an inconceivably intricate constellation of degradable parts, what else—given enough time—would our body and mind do? The instigating trouble may have begun yesterday, or it may have lain dormant for decades: an uneven growth spurt, Camp Lejeune waters, my colleague's tumor and multiple myeloma—asleep inside us, until it awakens. The body comes into focus as a time-traveling, memory-charged vessel, and the scary part is this. Our minds have virtually no access to this long-developing etiological drama. As Bessel van der Kolk tellingly entitled his study, "the body keeps the score." No doubt it does, but it is often only decades later that we discover that score—not to mention the nature of the game that, all unknowing, we had been playing, and eventually losing.

DORMANCY: MIND DRAMAS

I turn now to the central claims in my brother's talk, as he focused on "The Bear," the major story in *Go Down, Moses*. His two main points were interwoven. The first is that Faulkner's protagonist, Ike McCaslin, is engaged in reading his scene: reading bear tracks, decoding half-illegible ledgers (written before he was born, by his father and his uncle), grasping the stakes of his family's—and his region's—repeated acts of miscegenation. It takes Ike years to decode these cryptic signs of racial abuse and understand the injustice they bear witness to.

My brother's second point was that, over sixty years ago and in parallel fashion, we undergraduates were likewise engaged in (mis)reading our own scene. Like Faulkner's Ike, most of us could not decode, then, what was hidden in plain sight. We failed to grasp the structured racial politics that ensured that a token few Black students (less than five) had been admitted into our freshman class of 750. No less, coming from segregated Memphis, my brother and I could not see, then, how much it meant that the Black kids who lived near our public high school had never been allowed to attend it. We didn't grasp what our never seeing such kids (in school or out) was "saying." When do you come to understand that what you never lay your eyes on is something socially designed to be absent from your vision? We had become better readers since. Those earlier experiences lay dormant in us—until the social motives shaping them could no longer be concealed, and we started to wake up.

My brother focused on "The Bear," and I will turn soon to "Delta Autumn," a later story from *Go Down, Moses*. Ike McCaslin is the central figure of both stories. To help you understand what happens to him in the later story, I need to rehearse Ike's crucial move in "The Bear." He renounces his inheritance. But one must read carefully if one would understand why he does so. None of Ike's family understands his renunciation. The reasons remain concealed, legible only—if one would work to decode them—in the half-indecipherable ledgers kept by his father and his uncle. Those ledgers seem to show only that long before Ike was born, his widowed grandfather, Carothers McCaslin, traveled from northern Mississippi to New Orleans, where he bought a young slave named Eunice at the slave auction. On his return home he married Eunice off to one of his slaves, and she soon bore a daughter named Tomasina. Twenty-three years later, this same Tomasina gave birth to a boy named Turl. But why, six months before Turl's birth, would Tomasina's mother Eunice enter the nearby stream in order to drown herself? Ike's father cannot fathom her reasons, though it seems that Ike's uncle can. To the father's ledger-entry stating that Eunice "Drownd in Crick Cristmas Day 1832," the uncle revises him by writing, "Drownd herself." A bit later, Ike's bewildered father writes in response, "who in hell ever heard of a n***** drownding him self." The uncle's next ledger entry just repeats his claim: "Drownd herself."

Inscrutable ledgers, hidden motives, dead scribes, white reluctance to grant Black people full humanity (could a slave even *become* distraught enough to choose to end her life?): These are the obstacles to Ike's understanding. But he remembers that Turl looked unmistakably part white. And he ponders the other phrase in the ledgers—"father's will"—a phrase instructing the old man's sons to bequeath one thousand dollars to Turl once he came of age. Why would Ike's grandfather do that?

Eventually, Ike decodes this prehistory: First, the widowed Carothers McCaslin went to New Orleans to buy a young female slave to ease his loneliness. Next, he married her off to another slave, but the child she soon bore—Tomasina—was his. Twenty-three years later, Tomasina gave birth to Turl. Within this narrative frame, Eunice's drowning in the river six months before Turl's birth suddenly reveals a devastating time-logic: The mother kills herself when she discovers her daughter is three months pregnant—and more, impregnated by the white man who was her own father. Grasping this, Ike now envisages it all:

> He seemed to see her actually walking into the icy creek on that Christmas day six months before her daughter's and her lover's (*Her first lover's* he thought. *Her first*) child was born, solitary, inflexible, griefless, ceremonial, in formal and succinct repudiation of grief and despair who had already had to repudiate belief and hope.

"Fathers will" indeed—the ledgers record a bequest the old man would never pay in person, to a child he would never acknowledge as his own. So it falls to Ike to carry out the old man's "will." The bequest is too late for Turl, but not for his three offspring—James, Fonsiba, and Lucas. Ike gives Lucas and Fonsiba their inheritance, but James has disappeared.

All this is the background lying dormant for *Go Down, Moses*'s later story, "Delta Autumn." By now Ike, in his eighties, wants only to enjoy what may be his last hunt. He long ago gave up his inheritance, after discovering the racial abuse that inheritance was built upon. The precious thing that remains to him, though, is the wilderness and the two-week hunting ritual within it that he and the younger men conduct every November.

Hoping to get through his old age without further distress, Ike would love to not wake up one morning—and best of all, for this to happen at the wilderness camp. But Faulkner has one more life-altering encounter in store for him. That first morning at the wilderness camp, his surly great-nephew, Roth, enters Ike's tent and hands him an envelope. He tells Ike to give it to a messenger who will be coming—and if she asks for anything more, to say no. Soon enough, a white-skinned woman arrives at the wilderness camp, carrying a swaddled newborn baby.

The baby is Roth's, of course, and Ike dutifully hands the mother the envelope full of payoff cash. "That's just money," she tells him, to which he rejoins, "What else did you expect?" She goes on to tell Ike about the struggles of her own family, how they would take in washing to supplement their meager income:

> "Took in what?" he [Ike] said. "Took in washing?" . . . He cried, not loud, in a voice of amazement, pity, and outrage: "You're a n*****!"
> "Yes," she said. "James Beauchamp—you called him Tennie's Jim though he had a name—was my grandfather."

"Took in washing." No Southern white family in the early twentieth century would stoop to that form of work: That's what Black people were for. The woman is not only Black, but the granddaughter of the long-lost Tennie's Jim. Miscegenation and the lack of acknowledgment that follows from it, the proffering of money instead of love: from Carothers McCaslin in 1807 to Roth Edmonds in the 1940s, white men in Ike's family have slept with the Black women they owned or made into their mistresses—and then cast them out.

Distraught by this encounter, Ike pleads with the woman to go north, to marry a Black man. But as she is starting to leave the tent, he bids her to stop:

> "Wait:" although she had not turned, still stooping, and he put out his hand. But, sitting, he could not complete the reach until she moved her hand, the single hand which held the money, until he touched it. He didn't grasp it, he merely touched it—the gnarled, bloodless, bone-light bone-dry old man's fingers touching for a second the smooth young flesh where the strong old blood ran after its long lost journey home. "Tennie's Jim," he said. "Tennie's Jim."

So much is at stake in this touching of the two hands. Ike is "recovering" the long-missing Tennie's Jim, and he is honoring that "recovery." The full weight of his dormant, racially disfigured family history now lands upon him: a recognition in equal measure precious and unbearable. Faulkner seems to have understood something like this as well, for—though Ike has cameo appearances in Faulkner's subsequent novels—his capacity for change (for *drama*) is effectively exhausted. Ike remains hereafter immured, as it were, in the enormity of his "Delta Autumn" self-understanding.

I have needed space to spell out the intricate skein of recognitions occurring here—those of Ike within the narrative, those of the reader outside it. Three hundred pages separate this "Delta Autumn" moment from the one on which the novel opens: Buck and Uncle Buddy cheerfully chasing their young slave Turl, as he breaks away to join his sweetheart, Tennie, the property of a nearby landowner. No reader of *Go Down, Moses* has any idea, in these first pages, how much will be seen, eventually, to have been in play in that opening moment. Buck and Buddy will have taken on resonance; Turl will have become radioactive with resonance.

You'll note that I'm stressing the future and future perfect tenses—"will be seen," "will have taken on," "will have become"—for this is the larger temporal terrain on which both reading and life itself play themselves out. One of the central dramas of our life—as of Ike's—is our coming to understand later what was really going on earlier. Though we live our life as an ongoing present, we access its meanings only by way of those other tenses—the future when we will make our discoveries, the past whose concealed burdens we will come to understand. What better terms for such a time-saturated process of recognitions than dormancy and awakening?

To awaken what long lay dormant takes time. Likewise—and this may sound like a change of subject, but it is not—it is essential that *reading* lengthy narratives takes time as well. Indeed, so much time that many of today's undergraduates are fleeing from reading-intensive majors like English and the foreign languages, like history, religion, and philosophy. In a recent article in *The New Yorker*, entitled "The End of the English Major," Nathan Heller cited a Harvard professor musing, "The last time I taught *The Scarlet Letter*, I discovered that my students were really struggling to understand the sentences as sentences—like, having trouble identifying the subject and the verb." We know as well that more and more young people are incapable of writing cursive—which means incapable of *writing*.

Astounding as these developments may be, they should perhaps not surprise us. Shakespeare noted long ago that "my nature is subdu'd / To what it works in, like the dyer's hand" (Sonnet 111). It follows that the young cannot "work" cost-free, stain-free—unaffected—in a mediatic realm dominated by Twitter, TikTok, Instagram, and the like. In this realm, language acts typically vary in length from three seconds to ten minutes. More, the linguistic usages that accommodate this reduced time frame are cruelly deformed: u for you, r for are, b4 for before, etc. For me at least, the necessity of constructing text messages with one finger or thumb (or, for the more dexterous, two thumbs) is so repellant that I resort to it only when there is no alternative. Repellant because what can be said in these ways compares to genuine acts of communication as half a dozen notes on the piano would compare to a page of chamber music. I know the answer to my complaint: that the purpose is not the articulate-ness of the communication but its speed. What is wanted is *now*, better yet with pictures included. Making more of *now* is wonderful indeed, and no doubt even greater technological capacity to enlarge and extend the reach of *now* is coming our way. But *long-term* is no less wonderful. And *long-term* has the added appeal of being not just the condition under which our lives unfold over time. It is also the condition that bestows on us our best chance of figuring out who we were—and are.

I close with the third of the inquiries spawned by my brother's talk: what is at stake when "lecturees" become lecturers. Watching my brother talk to my classmates, I thought about how incapable all of us were, back then, of giving such a lecture. Without exception, the elderly speakers in this series are drawing on a lifetime of experiences, sifted and condensed into the form of a sixty-minute talk. We have, for good or ill, eventually figured out a number of things. We had to be immersed in those things for a lot of time—confused and stimulated, long in the dark but in search of light—before we could make our report. Dormant experiences take time to reveal their payload; they refuse the confines of Twitter and its cohorts.

You may recall the last words of that brilliant talker, Shakespeare's Hamlet: "The rest is silence." We older ones are acutely aware that the end is not so far off, and it will be speechless. Until then, though, we have something to say, and I do not speak of "organ recitals." However pressing old age's problems, one of its treasures is the awakening—unchosen, often upsetting—from dormancy, the fall into "this is your life" recognitions. Illness and insight, pain and perception, mistake and correction: These are not the exclusive property of the elderly. But they are never keener, more dramatic, more moving, than in our last chapters. Of course, none of the young would trade their youth for the discoveries coming our way. Nor should they. There is no rush. In due time they will get here, as we did, and find out for themselves.

THE THING ITSELF

"Thou art the thing itself; unaccommodated man is no more but such a poor, bare, forked animal as thou art." (Lear on the heath, gazing at mad Edgar, in *King Lear*)

A book focused on aging and the approach of death must finally come to "the thing itself." Lear's phrase is resonant, suggesting a stark, unprovided bodily core, shorn of accommodation. Let us begin by taking "the thing itself" literally: The human being, in its ultimate stage, reduces to mere "thingness," nothing but an animal body.

This "thing," once extinguished, is what we put into the coffin, and it is not hard to recognize the spatial and temporal pathway toward that final box. Anyone who has cared for declining parents likely knows the sequence: from their own comfortable home, to smaller but still acceptable rooms in a retirement community ("independent living"), then to fewer, barer rooms ("assisted living"), and finally to the smallest accommodation on offer, that unmistakably purposed last room with a bed at its center (little else needed), in the nursing unit of the community. I remember tracking my mother-in-law's ongoing "unaccommodation" by way of her ever-diminishing quarters. It was speechlessly clear—to my wife and me as we visited her—that this latest room would be her last, before her final resting place in the coffin. Or, via cremation, she would (as it turned out she did) ultimately occupy a smaller space yet.

Most aging humans participate in this material drama, as the body moves toward extinction. They know that they are in the process of becoming "unaccommodated." Usually this drama remains silent, often wrapped in shame as well. I recall such a shame-suffused scene with my father near the end. He was in a hospital room, and at one point—his shirt off and the age-lines on his body markedly visible, no one else in the room—he saw me looking at him and said, "You've never seen me like this before, have you?" No longer a subject—an I-who-can—he had become an object: a "me" observed and assessed by others. I could feel his humiliation that he had come to such a pass; there was no answer I could make. I noted as well that when hospital assistants would pick him up to carry him into the bathroom, he avoided eye contact with either them or us. It was as close as he could come to invisibility, not being there.

Late in my mother's life, she made an (unaccompanied) trip from her home in Memphis to a medical clinic in St. Louis. Her aim—which she found difficult to discuss with her three sons—was to participate in a discreet trial-experiment that might postpone her transition from underwear to diapers. Diapers: we begin our life in them, and if we live long enough, we will probably end our life in them. As babies, we never noticed; as old men and women, we are deeply embarrassed. The diapers signify that rather than beings best understood as a unique cluster of thoughts and feelings, we are becoming identifiable on a generic basis: bodies in need of diapers. The center of gravity seems to have changed: no longer the head and the heart, but the excretory areas, front and rear. That there's nothing personal about this is an assessment both welcome and intolerable. Welcome because at least it's not our fault, intolerable because our body parts no longer answer to our will: It's out of our hands.

Our center of gravity *seems* to have changed, I claim just above. If it had fully changed, there would be no embarrassment. Our pets show no shame at their excretory requirements. They are concerned, once trained, to do these things in the proper places; but that requirement met, they go about their business without squirming. We humans are not so carefree; our decreasing control of bladder and sphincter contributes massively to the humiliation inflicted by old age. To become incapable of disguising the needs of our failing bodies is both inevitable and unbearable.

Why humiliating? Why unbearable? Lear's term "unaccommodated" may shed further light. Those familiar with the play may remember the quietly harrowing earlier scene in which the old man, having given half his kingdom to each of his elder daughters, haggles with them as to the size of his permitted retinue of servants, now that he has yielded his crown and will be spending time in their quarters. The daughters, Goneril and Regan, keep reducing the number that he needs—from one hundred to fifty to twenty-five to ten or five and finally to one. Then they declare that he needs none at all since he will be amply supported by their servants. Furious, as he begins to grasp the terms of his mounting unaccommodation, Lear cries out:

O, reason not the need! Our basest beggars
Are in the poorest thing superfluous.
Allow not nature more than nature needs,
Man's life is cheap as beast's.

If it were only a question of meeting the body's needs, then mere nature would suffice—and man's life would be cheap as beast's. My father's averted gaze as he was being carried to the bathroom—like my mother's distressed journey from underwear to diapers—was certainly about need, but it was also about something more than need. Like Lear in dismay, they were suffering the loss of dignity that the coming end imposes. We make our lives meaningful by accommodations that transform animal nature into human nature. These accommodations may start as the dwellings we inhabit (homes: so much more than mere shelters from the rain and wind), but they go further: into social realms like dining (which converts mere feeding of the body into something more), clothing (a realm involving more than simply covering the body, and one superfluous for animals), as well as a host of group-inculcated ceremonies, projects, norms, and traditions that socialize our nature and make it human.

Perhaps above all, such accommodations include the sustaining realms of trust, friendship, and love. The faltering body, the need for diapers: These signaled to my aging parents a blow to their social identity itself. They registered the blow as a sign of their diminishment, and of further mortifications to come.

"The thing itself," the unaccommodated body, the failing flesh destined for the coffin. No one who is not a child can keep from knowing that this end is coming. All the chapters of my book have sought to explore the dramas that enrich—when they do not beset—the late stages of our journey. But the journey's end is mute: it cannot be written. As Hamlet's final words attest, "the rest is silence." I pivot now on Hamlet, for he provides the turn to literary testimony that this chapter takes. Hamlet's silence may join the silence common to all deaths, yet the Hamlet that matters is the uniquely speaking character written by Shakespeare. It is we the living who peer into the abyss—and none does this more memorably than Shakespeare—we who leave our testimony behind. I conclude this inquiry into the mind's responses to oncoming death by attending to two realms of creative pushback—humor and pathos.

HUMOR

The precariousness of "the thing itself"—the body headed for death—makes it an inexhaustible source of humor. Just think back on the involuntary chuckle likely to erupt from us when we catch ourselves from tripping on the stairs. This is humor in a double sense: the body as a set of humors, the body as a source of humor. Indeed, a considerable portion of medieval medical practice was founded on a theory of bodily humors. Blood (sanguine), black bile (melancholic), yellow bile (choleric), and phlegm (phlegmatic)—elements present in varying proportions, they believed, in every human body—were understood to underwrite human identity. Excesses or deficiencies of any of these would explain the "humoral" imbalance that manifested as eccentricity or illness.

It may be less far-fetched than it seems to align the theory of the body as composed of humors with an art of the body as humorous. Both are based on collapse—the likelihood of a coming fall. If we think back to the comic films of Chaplin and Keaton, a central recurring event is the pratfall. That is the moment when a gesticulating standing figure suddenly lands on his backside. That these films are silent is no limitation. The pratfall "announces" that the protestations of speech are mere surface; the deeper point is the body's fall. That is the (silent) comeuppance revealing the character's foundational identity as bodily, all verbal claptrap notwithstanding. The body is generic—"the thing itself," the thing that falls. If we would decode the pratfall, it might read something like this: Make whatever claims you wish; your essential creatureliness—what is fallible and funny about you—will be expressed in your fall. You will come a cropper; everyone does eventually. The low slang French phrase for pretentious behavior is "il pète plus haut que son cul" ("he farts higher than his asshole"). When the human animal preens, a reckoning and reminder are due.

The pratfall and diapers, the backside and the asshole: These "tell" a different story than the loquacious mouth. No one has written this different story more trenchantly than the twentieth-century playwright and novelist Samuel Beckett. Here is his protagonist, Molloy, rehearsing the failure of his own body and, while at it, the underappreciated significance of the rectum:

> I apologize for having to revert to this lewd orifice, 'tis my muse will have it so. . . . We underestimate this little hole, it seems to me, we

call it the arse-hole and affect to despise it. But is it not rather the true portal of our being and the celebrated mouth no more than the kitchen-door? Nothing goes in, or so little, that is not rejected on the spot, or very nearly. Almost everything revolts it that comes from without and what comes from within does not seem to receive a very warm welcome either.

The rectum as the true portal of our being: What might that entail? First, that we overestimate the value of the claims tirelessly issuing from our upper mouth. Who is listening anyway, and for how long? More, the lower mouth's field of operations "corrects" the upper mouth's pretentions. This lower one has a good deal less to say, and none of it is welcome. That mouth doesn't (for the most part) like things to enter it, and others rarely take kindly to what exits from it. In fact, its entire ambiance is revolting: You can build no social cohesion out of a gathering of assholes. An offensive stench is the only common factor—the stench of decaying matter. Humankind the world over heading to the tomb, shitting, pissing, farting on the way. To emphasize the role of the rectum would be to acknowledge the omnipresence of shit that covers the globe. On this model, the human being is no longer "homo faber," but rather "homo excrementum"—not man the maker but man the shitter. Or, perhaps more accurately, the one who has been shat. Molloy imagines himself as having been shat out by his mother, "her who brought me into the world, through the hole in her arse if my memory is correct. First taste of the shit."

There is no serious plotting in Beckett's fictional world. Vladimir and Estragon are theoretically waiting for Godot, but Godot remains scrupulously absent from the scene. No transforming future event is on the horizon; there is no horizon. Beckett's theatrical settings are better described as a quagmire or quicksand than as a field of anticipations. They are entirely unaccommodating. The last spoken line of *Waiting for Godot* is "Yes, let's go." The stage direction beneath it reads, "They do not move." Nagg and Nell (in *Endgame*) are truncated bodies stuck inside trash cans and only able to move their heads. And, of course, to talk: Beckett's people talk inexhaustibly, even as they have nothing fruitful to say.

Why, you might ask, would anyone find this interesting? Let me try to answer the question, knowing that most playgoers vote with their feet and keep a distance from his plays, even as most readers ignore his fiction.

Yet Beckett's testimony is precious. If you believe (as he seems to) that language serves as humankind's supreme means of deceiving itself, then the plotting/becoming/cohering that language insists on must somehow be exposed. For Beckett, the truths of the body and of the mind are obvious and incontestable. The body is a machine that is endlessly falling apart, on its way to final collapse, while the mind is an energy forever committed to language games promoting fantasies of Coherence. In *Molloy*, Beckett actually allows one sentence to credibly articulate this logic: "There could be no things but nameless things, no names but thingless names." If I have this right, Beckett is saying, through Molloy, that physical things are real and exist in their own sphere, and verbal names are likewise real and exist in their own sphere. But these two spheres—which we continuously superimpose upon each other if we would make sense of our world— remain separate. The things we know to exist do not fit the names we proclaim for them; they remain nameless. The names we insist on have no purchase on the things they pretend to enclose and identify; they remain thingless. As bodied beings, we do not escape—whatever we may say—the comic plight of unaccommodation that is our thing-fate.

If the above is true (and I recognize the fragility of any claim with respect to Beckett's intentions), then his own language must keep expressing the misfit between the "intentional" way his people talk and the embodied trouble they are in. Hamm and Clov, Vladimir and Estragon, the characters in Beckett's fiction: They all speak past each other, and nothing they say can bring their physical troubles to resolution. Beckett's genius is to create the language for saying such imbroglios—a verbal world always about to undermine its own representational premises, to pull out the rug it has just seemed to put under the reader's feet. A passage from *Molloy* may make this point clearer. Molloy says: "My boots. They came up to where my calves would have been if I had had calves, and partly they buttoned, or would have buttoned, if they had had buttons." A bit later, on the same page, Molloy is having trouble riding his bicycle: "But I pushed and pulled in vain, the wheels would not turn. It was as though the brakes were jammed, and heaven knows they were not, for my bicycle had no brakes." As readers we want to go along; we want to credit those boots and calves and buttons and brakes. That's what reading means: trusting the linguistic representation eventually to make sense, and imaginatively going where it is taking us. So what is happening here? Are we just being toyed with? This unpredictable playing—when fiction suddenly undercuts its representations and reveals that it is "fiction"—occurs as well in the following duet in *Endgame*. Clov says to Hamm, "I'll leave you," and Hamm responds, "No!" Clov rejoins, "What is there to keep me here?" to which Hamm answers, "The dialogue." The dialogue: Hamm concedes that they are merely actors performing scripted characters named Clov and Hamm. If you are an inveterate playgoer, you may recoil at this breaking of trust: A character must remain, if not *in* character, then at least *a* character! But perhaps there is a part of your mind that thinks, well, these *are* actors playing at being Clov and Hamm. What might it mean for the playwright to invite you to ponder the fictionality of his fiction—to feel it as both appeal and illusion? Throughout Beckett's work, that is the part of your mind he is trying to reach—perhaps so that you might begin to ponder the appeal and illusion of your own fictions.

Humor, pratfalls, the body: these "express" the comic collapse of higher purposes. Beckett's prose deftly avoids the temptation to take its own plotting seriously. Put better, it "knows" that bodied troubles (the constipated Krapp; Hamm, who can't walk; Clov, who can't sit; Winnie, who is buried up to her neck in the sand) are immune to the fantasy of plot-cures, that it is a waste of everyone's time to pretend otherwise. His work is invested in insoluble physical dilemmas—wittily, zanily so—which is why I have turned to him here. More than any other writer I know, he is using language to call into question language's most seductive suasions of Significance. His characters may say yes, let's go, as often as they like. But the thing itself—the unaccommodated body—remains motionless. We are in endgame territory, where, at the end of the play, "they do not move."

And yet, and yet: Beckett's wry comedy comes at us not as a submission to "the thing itself"—to silence and eventual extinction—but as a saucy, impudent act of life. *It* is what moves. Humor may be of the body and explain why we are done for, but "humor" is of the mind, and it delights in this hilarious state of affairs. A Chaplin pratfall expresses likewise the mind's failure to control the body, and the mind's (ours as we watch) delight in being thus reminded. It does so by turning a fall into a kind of dance, yet without ceasing to remain a fall. A Beckett play does something kindred.

PATHOS

Where Shakespeare goes with the tragedy of *King Lear* is more remarkable yet. The play's refusal of consolation (repetitions of "nothing" and "never" sound the play's bass notes) puts before the viewer a haunting enactment of life's darkest possibilities. So dark, indeed, that Shakespeare's seventeenth-century editor Nahum Tate's brighter version of the play held the stage for 150 years, from 1681 well into the nineteenth century. Tate certainly patched things up: In his revision of Shakespeare's play, Cordelia marries Edgar, and all ends well. Almost a century after Tate's intervention, Samuel Johnson (an editor working with the play as Shakespeare actually intended it) confessed that he understood why audiences preferred Tate. "I was many years ago so shocked by Cordelia's death that I know not whether I ever endured to read again the last scenes of the play." "The thing itself"— Cordelia's dead body—is unbearable to behold. Rather than keep her alive and thus satisfy an audience's desire to limit the destruction that Lear himself has set in motion, Shakespeare went the other way. He wrote the anguish Cordelia's father felt in confronting the loss of what he should have held dearest. Gazing upon her dead body, Lear speaks these awful words:

Why should a dog, a horse, a rat, have life,
And thou no breath at all? Thou'lt come no more,
Never, never, never, never, never!

Never: our greatest writers take us into the presence of what can hardly be borne—but *can* be written. I close this chapter by turning to a slow-motion unfolding of a kindred recognition. This is the silently shocking moment when Proust's Marcel suddenly sees death's mark on his sick grandmother's beloved face. Her voice had sounded strange when he phoned her, so to ease his anxiety he has come to her home, unannounced. (Unannounced, as we shall see, makes all the difference.) The passage needs to be quoted at length:

> Alas, it was this phantom that I saw when, entering the drawing-room before my grandmother had been told of my return, I found her reading. I was in the room, or rather I was not yet in the room since she was not aware of my presence, and, like a woman whom one surprises at a piece of needlework which she will hurriedly put aside if anyone comes in, she was absorbed in thoughts which she had never allowed to be seen

by me. Of myself—thanks to that privilege which
does not last but which gives one, during the brief
moment of return, the faculty of being suddenly
the spectator of one's own absence—there was
present only the witness . . . the stranger who
does not belong to the house, the photographer
who has called to take a photograph of places
which one will never see again. The process
that automatically occurred in my eyes when
I caught sight of my grandmother was indeed
a photograph. We never see the people who
are dear to us save in the animated system, the
perpetual motion of our incessant love for them,
which before allowing the images that their faces
present to reach us, seizes them in its vortex
and flings them back upon the idea that we have
always had of them, makes them adhere to it,
coincide with it. How, since into the forehead
and the cheeks of my grandmother I had been
accustomed to read all the most delicate, the
most permanent qualities of her mind, how, since
every habitual glance is an act of necromancy,
each face that we love a mirror of the past, how
could I have failed to overlook what had become

dulled and changed in her? . . . But if, instead of
our eyes, it should happen to be a purely physical
object, a photographic plate, that has watched the
action, then what we see, in the courtyard of the
Institute, for example, instead of the dignified
emergence of an Academician who is trying to hail
a cab, will be his tottering steps, his precautions
to avoid falling on his back, the parabola of his
fall, as though he were drunk or the ground
covered in ice. So it is when some cruel trick
of chance prevents our intelligent and pious
tenderness from coming forward in time to hide
from our eyes what they ought never to behold . . .
and they, arriving first in the field and having it to
themselves, set to work mechanically, like films,
and show us, in place of the beloved person who
has long ago ceased to exist but whose death our
tenderness has always hitherto kept concealed
from us, the new person whom a hundred times
daily it has clothed with a loving and mendacious
likeness. And . . . I, for whom my grandmother
was still myself, I who had never seen her save
in my own soul, always in the same place in the
past, through the transparency of contiguous and

overlapping memories, suddenly . . . for the first
time and for a moment only, since she vanished
very quickly, I saw, sitting on the sofa beneath the
lamp, red-faced, heavy and vulgar, sick, vacant,
letting her slightly crazed eyes wander over a
book, a dejected old woman whom I did not know.

What is Marcel seeing here? First, he sees that our
normal seeing of those we love is a reciprocal pact rather
a private activity, and therefore without guarantee, the
pact liable to collapse. All his former acts of seeing his
grandmother had been conditioned upon a reciprocal
seeing-back that underwrote their value: the two of them
acknowledging each other. This love-enabled mutuality
is the precious thing: He remains her Marcel so long as
she remains his grandmother. But her bodily insertion in
outer space and ongoing time makes her a being continuously altering and materially unreachable—an intolerable
situation that we normally repress from consciousness.
But not here. Looking at her not seeing him, he becomes
"the spectator of [his] own absence." Literally, he is not
there in her field of vision; more deeply, he is *not there*
unless sanctioned by her love for him. Uncorroborated
by her, he gazes at his own absence; he has suddenly

become "the stranger who does not belong to the house." Deprived of her sponsorship, he momentarily ceases to be.

The passage of time—no longer kept at bay—lurches into view, and Marcel realizes that for the longest time he has not been seeing his actual grandmother. He has all along been "overlooking" her, "overlooking" time's impact on her body and mind. But in this charged moment—his eyes now functioning like an impersonal, time-sensitive photographic lens—he *sees* her. The pathos of the passage is that it takes his grandmother *not* seeing him for him to see her as she actually is: now. Such unbearable seeing lasts, mercifully, but a moment. The curtain drops; habit regains its sway; she reappears as she has always appeared, as she used to be.

Who has not experienced that shocking moment when, seeing someone dear whom you haven't seen for some time, you suddenly—and for a second only—recognize the death-journey written on their face? I shall never forget visiting my mother once, shortly after a flight she had taken came close to crashing. She was not looking at me, as I lingered on her face, and I suddenly grasped the impersonal reality of her age, the meaning of all those stress-lines, her unbridgeable spatial distance from me.

No matter the strength of my love, I could do nothing to alter those telltale marks and the journey they testified to. How we normally see those we love—reciprocally and therefore blindly—remains blessedly out of date, years behind the facts available on the implacable calendar. Proust likens such habits of abiding misrecognition to "acts of necromancy," a kind of black magic in which, as in a séance, we see (as though alive) someone dear who is actually dead. I know of no writer more attuned than Proust to the invisible and transforming traffic that occurs in something as apparently simple as looking at one you love. It is the love that does the heavy work of concealment and transformation.

The analogy proposed at the end of the quote—the tottering academician (headed for a pratfall)—points to a male subject, Marcel rather than his grandmother. But the deeper identity being graphed here is neither Marcel's alone nor his grandmother's alone. What we come away with is an exquisitely intersubjective compact—the love-fueled dance that is Marcel-and-his-grandmother, symbiotic to the highest degree. The passage moves us because it spells out with extraordinary delicacy how we live by way of the unthinking endorsement of others, and how they likewise live by way of ours.

The thing itself—as Beckett, Shakespeare, and Proust all show—is never merely itself. Whoever is dying, even if (as often in Beckett) it is the speaker himself, someone is irrepressibly talking. Someone is memorably—comically, tragically, poignantly—registering the damage being inflicted. Whether it be Lear's heartbroken speech in the presence of the dead Cordelia, or Beckett's Hamm envisaging his extinction, or Marcel gazing upon his doomed grandmother, someone is speaking. That speaking may be wry or painful or suffused with the helplessness of a bystander. Regardless, it registers our response to death's indifferent power.

Death itself remains dumb. It takes us, the (still) living, to make death speak. As Yeats puts it, man "knows death to the bone— / Man has created death." The fact of dying has been around ever since life began, but the idea of death is probably available only to humans. It is a supreme idea—that we are both cursed and blessed to know in advance that we will die—and there is no limit to the number of enterprises it has inspired. My book has been intent on exploring several of these, and it may be appropriate to repeat a claim made in my opening chapter. If it is a commonplace that we do not know what to do with death, it is no less true that we would not know what to do without it. Destined to remove all breath, it breathes life into our creative endeavors.

FREE

An earlier chapter of this book raided Wallace Stevens's poem "Sunday Morning" for the phrase that would serve as its title: "The Mother of Beauty." That chapter explored the approach of death as generative in ways that have nothing to do with "fulfillment." Indeed, there is no gainsaying the disturbing force of incapacitation awaiting the elderly. Yet Stevens's female protagonist in "Sunday Morning" seems far from anguished about what will be coming her way. Rather than piously spend her Sunday mornings in church—so as to convert the menace of eventual bodily extinction into religious transcendence—she relishes the abundant time in the bedroom, the unrushed unfolding of sensuous pleasures: "Complacencies of the peignoir, and late / Coffee and oranges in a sunny chair." Late morning rituals, a currying of the body, with coffee and oranges and sunshine on offer: This—rather than "the holy hush of ancient sacrifice"—is the Sunday morning scenario she dwells on. What is such a leisurely ceremony doing in a poem concerned with human mortality? Doesn't she know it will all end badly?

Oddly enough, my wife and I—both of us in our mid-eighties—may have come up with an answer. Although we both know perfectly well that it will all end badly, we indulge in a daily drama (not just Sundays!) that echoes the matutinal one envisaged in Stevens's poem. Except for the day or two of the week when one of us has a mandatory morning commitment—alarm clock days, these—I awaken on my own and quietly get out of bed around 8 a.m. Then, not to disturb my wife's slumber, I tiptoe out of our bedroom and head toward the kitchen. (Our new master bedroom is downstairs—same floor as the kitchen. This move downstairs is an alteration prompted—in advance of being necessitated—by our increasing age.) Once in the kitchen, I focus on brewing a pot of coffee, using the special beans that a friend's son-in-law roasts and sells on our island. I then load a tray with two mugs of steaming coffee—and perhaps a pastry or two if there happen to be fresh ones in our pantry—and I make my way back to the bedroom. Most days this works like a charm. My almost-awake wife will have heard the sound of the grinding coffee beans, will have roused and made herself presentable. She will have fluffed up the pillows on her side of our bed (I will have done my side earlier, in anticipation), awaiting my arrival. (She cannot function, later, without that initial cup of coffee; she likes it best in bed.) Every now and then she sleeps through the modest sounds of my rising, leaving, and bean-grinding. No problem: After preparing the coffee, I glance into our bedroom to see if she's propped up in the bed or still out flat and dreaming. If the latter, I leave the coffee in the pot—where it will stay hot for as long as needed—and walk into my study (one room over) to check the predicted weather and overnight email. Within twenty or thirty minutes at most, my wife awakens. That is my cue: I rise from the computer, return to the kitchen, then come to the bed with two mugs of coffee (and maybe the odd croissant). That's when our ritual begins.

It unfolds like this. We sit next to each other in bed and, for the first few minutes, do little other than sip the hot coffee. Words are gathering in each of us, but there is no rush to speak them. We have at our disposal, as well, a lovely scene to look out on. From our bed we see the downward sweep of our property (two and a half acres, but it feels limitless from the perspective of the bed), and we gaze on the distant Vineyard Sound, a quarter mile away. There is often—even at that early hour—a sailboat or two moving in their stately fashion, perhaps a stationary fishing boat as well. We have no idea who is on these vessels and no interest in finding out. There is usually, as well, a gathering of familiar birds on the nearby trees—half of them probably waiting for my wife to take the hint and refill the bird feeder on the other side of our property. Every now and then a regal-looking hawk, his wings solemnly folded about him, perches motionlessly at the top of the big oak seventy-five yards away. He never remains there for long, and we wait for his sudden departure, hoping to see those great outstretched wings.

Eventually we begin our chat by returning to last night's events (a TV movie or series, or perhaps dinner with a few friends), whatever it was, now subject to further sifting. Or we might rehearse today's interests, such as the books we are halfway through and "invested" in enough to characterize for each other. Or the computer headlines I just read and am disturbed by enough to talk about now. Or what might be appealing for dinner tonight—and, once identified, whether we have its makings in the fridge or the freezer, or will need to drive to the grocery store. If, as often, a drive is required (we're a good twenty-five minutes away from the nearest grocery store), what else might get accomplished on that trek? Is this a good time to go down-island and look for Christmas presents for our kids and grandkids, maybe for each other as well? Or the right moment for buying another thirty pound bag of birdfeed? Perhaps a visit to the hardware store for more mousetraps? (The man who helps us look after our house informed us, some twenty-five years ago when we built it, that the mice were here before we came, and they will be here after we leave.) These casual conversations occur during that first cup of coffee and perhaps a refill; the ritual may take up as much as an hour. Eventually we take turns heading into the shower. It is time to get our day underway.

I call it a ritual, but the word "ceremony" is equally apt. When Yeats spoke of "the ceremony of innocence" in his 1919 poem "The Second Coming," he was imagining a stay against weighty menaces—the eruption of war, "the blood-dimmed tide." He could hardly have had in mind such modest rites as ours—unless perhaps he did? For there is something precious in the simplicity of these habitual moves we make almost every morning: the anticipation and then enactment of a sequence of inconspicuous life-activities together.

Just getting into the day, one might say—little doings familiar and available to everyone. Except that the young are too busy preparing to go to school even to imagine such a ritual (not that it would appeal to them if they had time for it). And the grown-ups are too busy getting the young off to school—and then themselves off to work—to consider the coffee-in-bed ceremony that launches the daily performance of our lives. Were the grown-ups somehow to have the time for it, they too would swiftly pass on our little ceremony. It would appear to them at best as a quaint displacement of more compelling tasks—fitting perhaps for the elderly, but trivial, even a touch perverse, for busy folks like them, still in the prime of their lives.

With their lives essentially in front of them, the young spring forward toward school and beyond (however they might complain about it). No less, the adults—their lives essentially in the making now—likewise head toward the jobs and responsibilities they've chosen for themselves (or found themselves caught up in). In both cases the time frame being lived through—childhood or adulthood—sanctions no time for a leisurely morning hour in bed together, sitting up and parsing what went on yesterday, what might be on the agenda for today. Our ritual is ours alone. At this point a strange recognition may spring into focus: It is only us, the old ones—not our children nor our grandchildren—whose time is entirely our own.

We who are, by definition, running toward empty, heading relentlessly out of time: We are the ones who, with virtually royal nonchalance, have all the time in the world at our disposal. There is nothing we have to do.

I have quoted Wallace Stevens already, and before I end, I shall quote Samuel Johnson. But the most eloquent gloss for this kind of wintry freedom comes from Shakespeare, *King Lear*, the last scene of Act V. It is relevant that the vision of freedom Lear describes to his daughter Cordelia is inseparable from the prison walls that close them in:

> No, no, no, no! Come, let's away to prison:
> We two alone will sing like birds i' the cage:
> When thou dost ask me blessing, I'll kneel down,
> And ask of thee forgiveness: so we'll live,
> And pray, and sing, and tell old tales, and laugh
> At gilded butterflies, and hear poor rogues
> Talk of court news; and we'll talk with them too,
> Who loses and who wins; who's in, who's out;
> And take upon 's the mystery of things,
> As if we were God's spies: and we'll wear out,
> In a walled prison, packs and sects of great ones,
> That ebb and flow by the moon.

The pathos of this moment is powerful. Had Lear been able to grasp, earlier, the late-stage freedom that his old age might have offered up to him—the intimacy with his daughter that only a yielding up of the throne and its responsibilities would have made possible—he might have spared himself and others the tragic events his behavior has launched. He might have accepted his last chapter—and found his way into a tranquility he never imagined. He and Cordelia as "birds i' the cage," yes: either the prison that Albany intends for them, or the foreclosed space that is the time of the aged with those they love. Here with Cordelia, beyond all the machinations of the royal court—"who loses and who wins; who's in, who's out"—Lear enters a blessed space freed from all wanting. What he wants is with him: his daughter Cordelia. Being this near to death, he envisages their taking on "the mystery of things, / As if we were God's spies."

To see in this most tragic of Shakespeare's plays a luminous moment of plenitude—Lear and Cordelia together, sprung free from the plots and counterplots of power—takes us away, of course, from the play's denouement. She will be hanged, and he will thus lose what he loves more than life: "never, never, never, never, never." The unbearableness of "never" is where the play is headed, Lear's intolerable unaccommodation. Yet this same passage lets us glimpse, if only briefly, the paradoxical fusion of freedom and necessity that I am claiming for old age itself. The prison walls bespeak the approaching end, but they also shelter a *beyond* that those outside its walls, bent on power and advancement, remain blind to: the *beyond* when there's nothing more you want, when you enjoy the miracle of what you have. A *beyond* that becomes a *here*. Is this the meaning of freedom itself? Though only a moment, it is one of plenitude, opening upon "the mystery of things."

The ritual my wife and I share of morning coffee in bed is surely far too humble for me to claim any access to "the mystery of things"! Neither of us would dream that we are God's spies. But we perhaps do grasp something that in its modest way may be a touch godlike: that our approaching death is the birthing condition of this new release into life. It is the key that opens the door for an experience of time that is, for now, full, unhurried, and free. It is, in its way, magical.

I mentioned Samuel Johnson earlier, and he now comes into play. His biographer, Boswell, quotes him as saying, "Depend upon it, sir. When a man knows he is to be hanged in a fortnight, it concentrates his mind wonderfully." Of course, my wife and I anticipate that we have a good deal more than a fortnight before the grim reaper appears, but we realize—as the young and the middle-aged do not—that he is actually on the way. Our calendars tell us this essential fact, however our hearts may deny it, our minds may elude it. Our increasingly faulty bodies tell us also—especially in the mirror. Other chapters in this book have been at pains to clarify that this is not good news. Recurrent forgetfulness (presages of dementia?), increasing bodily creakiness (signs of the cane to come, then the wheelchair?), all those funerals and memorial services for the departed whom we liked or loved (first drafts for our own memorial service, from which, at least, we will be blessedly absent, whatever the state of our body?): these are pressing hints, handwritings on the wall that even our faulty eyesight cannot keep from decoding. We know exactly where we are headed.

That the end is known—yet its meaning unknowable— is not surprising. Apart from the determined atheists and the unquenchably faithful, the rest of us tend to concede that where we're finally headed is an insoluble mystery. This book about time's bounty has nothing to say about possible realms beyond time. Its focus, instead, has been on our lives in time, for as I have aged, I now find no topic more interesting. Not time as the great philosophers might discuss it, but time as we prosaically live through it, change within it, and approach its cessation (for us). As Samuel Johnson grasped, the last chapter opens up "wonderfully" to the charged mind of one condemned to death in ten days. That could be the case for any of us—who escapes eventual extinction?—but our species tends to sustain the illusion that we will live forever. We know it is illusion, but we feel it as truth. A sort of all-protective fantasy, its payoff has been handsome, for it has, throughout the previous decades, underwritten our sanity itself.

Yet Johnson glimpsed—as the end comes increasingly into view—a concentration of the mind not otherwise available. The younger have no way of knowing that the impairments occasioned by aging—earlier projects on the wane or clean abandoned, children long gone, the body losing its resources, the mind starting to go gamey—might harbor in their train a purer enjoyment of time. The ritual my wife and I share of coffee in bed and the aimless chatter that accompanies it enacts our freedom. No company or institution or cause owns us. We are, however diminished, our own agents. Our daily ceremony partakes of undiluted presence. We will not stay in that bed all morning, but no pang of guilt moves through us during the half hour or hour of our coffee and conversation. Few calls intrude. For a while, doing nothing that anyone else would find remotely important, we are together, here, and free. That may not seem like much, and it may not last that long. But we never had it earlier, and for us it is enough.

ACKNOWLEDGMENTS

To begin with immediate indebtedness: David Allender, publisher of Godine Press, recognized at once—by way of my brief description of the project—that he would want to publish *Time's Bounty*. Such recognition is rare, and it led to a working relationship with Godine that has no equal in my experience. Celia Johnson, Senior Editor, engaged my argument—in painstaking detail—with an unfailing blend of generosity and acuity. Beth Blachman scrupulously copy-edited my manuscript, Virginia Downes took professional care of production, and Natalie Sousa's interior designs made *Time's Bounty* (whatever its other merits) something lovely to behold.

Three of my chapters enjoyed an earlier life as independent essays. I thank *Raritan* for permission to republish "The Mother of Beauty"; it appeared in their Winter 2023 issue. The essay "Less" first appeared in the Summer 2022 issue of *The Hedgehog Review* and is reprinted here with the permission of the publisher. *The American Scholar* published "Free" in its Fall 2024 issue and has given permission to reprint it here.

Less immediate forms of indebtedness go deeper. After publishing one of my essays, Jay Tolson, editor of *The Hedgehog Review*, went on to read the entire manuscript and to give me good advice. My old colleague, David Riggs—in another century we were instructors together at Harvard—judiciously commented on this book's argument, as he has done for the others I've written in the interim. My twin brother, Arnold, and I—both of us college professors—have shared, throughout our lives, our sense of what it means to be alive, as well as the fluctuating stakes of teaching, of writing, and of family.

My least immediate indebtedness is greatest and beyond repaying. My wife Penny has read and reread all that I have written, ever since I labored over fifty years ago (in a converted coal-scuttle in the basement of Harvard student housing) to complete a dissertation on Henry James. She and I have journeyed together into the country of old age. Without her unstinting bounty there would be no *Time's Bounty*, and I dedicate my book to her.

PERMISSIONS

A NOTE ABOUT
THE AUTHOR

© PENNY WEINSTEIN

Born in the South (Memphis, Tennessee), Philip Weinstein earned his bachelor's degree at Princeton and his doctorate at Harvard. For over 40 years he taught a wide range of literature (European, British, and American) at Swarthmore College. His major research focus has been the fiction of William Faulkner, and his *Becoming Faulkner* won the Hugh Holman Award as the best book on Southern literature published in 2010.

Since retirement, he and his wife live on Martha's Vineyard, where he continues to teach and to write. But now he attunes both activities to the aims and interests of the literate "common reader." To this end, his recent publications take the form of essays that rise from personal experience in order to shed light on broadly shared social realities. *Soul-Error* explores the subjective orientations operating upon our thoughts, expectations, and memories. *Time's Bounty* focuses on the territory that (if we live long enough) we come to inhabit: the remarkable territory of old age. Remarkable because, despite our preconceptions, it turns out to be chock-full of challenge and surprise.